Serial Killer Explanation

Written by

Darin Graves

https://www.theempirepublishers.com/

Our books may be purchased in bulk for promotional, educational, or business use.

Please contact The Empire Publishers at +1 844 636-4579, or by email at support@theempirepublishers.com

First Edition December 2025

About the Author

Darin Graves was born in Jamestown, North Dakota. His early years were marked by questions, challenges, and a sense of searching, but through it all, he never gave up. He later earned a degree in Psychology from North Dakota State University, a time in his life when things began to come together, until a life-altering incident nearly took everything away. After spending two weeks in a coma and three months in the hospital learning to walk again, Darin emerged with a new perspective and an unshakable determination to write.

Living with a traumatic brain injury hasn't stopped him from doing what he loves, writing novels that dive deep into the darker corners of the human psyche. "Time and patience," he says, have been his greatest tools. Now 59, he writes with clarity of mind and a passion for storytelling, even if the body has taken a few hits along the way.

Darin isn't one for long-winded prose. His novels are sharp, concise, and crafted to fill every narrative gap without unnecessary filler. With four novels already completed, this latest work stands apart, larger in scope and more cinematic in vision. Inspired by the perfection of The Exorcist, a film he calls hypnotic, Darin set out to create something in its spirit, but with his own unique twist. Instead of a demon like Pazuzu, this time, it's St. Lucifer himself watching over one of his most chilling creations: Mick.

All of Darin's novels are written with film adaptation in mind. He hopes readers, and producers, will see the cinematic potential within these pages.

Table of Contents

Preface

The serial killer plot has been used in novels correctly, incorrectly, altered, fixed, restyled, and remolded. I decided to take it a step further, find the cause. And individual murders another, why? What drives that action? In examining the cause, my personal and scientific approach points to something deeper: it's in the cells and neurons inside the brain. We're not talking about murder driven by financial gain, jealousy, or hatred. Serial killers murder due to a disoriented and malfunctioning brain nucleus. The killer is within them, environmental factors merely bring it to bear.

Let's talk about the Devil. There's an eerie calm in the way we sometimes speak of him, almost a quiet exhilaration and strange admiration for the fallen angel. We see him as evil, and we should. His hatred for humankind is clear. God sees humans as equal in life to angels and saints, preposterous! The fallen angel lingers in our minds. He must be the cause of war, murder, and all things dark. *Diablos!*

From *The Omen to The Exorcist*, the scent of divine wickedness and immoral acts feeds our fascination with evil. Do our psychological imaginations, those fanciful dances of the id, drive us to watch *The Silence of the Lambs?* We are aware of the iniquity in these characters, the bleak gestures of who they are, yet we still watch. Why? Stimulation? Novelty? The darker aspects of our minds trigger a fight-or-flight response. Fear and dread are served up like a cup of coffee, some people crave the frightening experience. Divine horror entertains us, satisfying our curiosity about the dark corners of the human psyche.

When watching horror, the viewer is physically safe; it's just a movie. Their safety frame remains intact. A psychotic killer chasing a bloodied victim exists only on the screen, but it still gives them pause. Actors and directors make these plots feel too real at times. But what happens when the lights go off and the credits roll? "Crap… I'm not getting any sleep tonight," the viewer mutters. "Make sure all the doors and windows are locked." Horror films tap into something primal. In the silence of night, alone in the dark, self-pity mixes with regret. "Shoot…what was that noise?"

I wrote this novel using neuroscience, psychology, and a spiritual overview. Yes, the Devil may have his own reasons, his own cause, for a serial killer's actions. This novel was incredibly fun to write. Don't ask me why. I'm a reasonable man. I wouldn't hurt a fly. I'm well-educated and use my own judgement to search for what I believe is the truth. Humanity's past is like any failing empire, violent and questionable. I hope the reader sees this. I embedded an engaging story and plot into the real causes of serial killing. Humans are predators. Our history proves it. Sadly, killing seems embedded in the cycle of life.

P.S.

This topic has haunted me for years. I'm 59 years old now, but back in high school, I kind of, sort of, watched a movie titled *The Exorcist*. Scared the hell out of me! I say "sort of watched" because I was petrified, nervous, agitated... and hiding under a little blanket whenever the demon spoke. I was both frightened and exhilarated by the power of imagination and the incredible craft behind it.

Even then, I knew this film, this motion picture, was the work of a genius. His name was William Friedkin. Rest in peace. I've watched several short films on the making of *The Exorcist*. Friedkin was a madman in the best way. He pushed Mercedes McCambridge, the voice of the demon, to reach terrifying levels of performance. He spent two months constructing a portion of the set just to make sure there was a window beneath the steps where the priest would fall to his death.

I read that when four studio executives previewed the film, one said, "It'll make millions." The other three said, "Lock it in a vault, fans can't handle this." Friedkin made other films I adore. *To Live and Die in L.A.* is one of my favorites.

But back to the point, my second novel started as a short story called *Mick*. I expanded it and called the result *Serial Killer Explanation*. For years, I've wanted to create something that could stand beside *The Exorcist*. I know, I've wasted time watching cheap knockoffs. Movies about demonic possession have become so ridiculously clichéd they belong in the comedy section, not horror. Did their directors not see the flaws?

I read *The Exorcist* four times. I watched the movie twenty. If nothing else, to study it. But I know now: it can't be replicated. I could never come close. It is flawless. Blatty's novel was a masterpiece. Friedkin's uncompromising direction made it perfect.

So I kept my little story, *Mick,* and I turned it into something new: a novel that explains the customs, habits, and psychological style of a serial killer. I had to include a priest, a detective, and yes, the Devil himself, as observers of the mind of a killer named Mick.

1

Serial Killer Explanation

"I kill her, and I will be fulfilled," I tell myself.

But it never happens.

So, the next woman, surely this time, it will happen, I'll be fulfilled. But no, it never does.

Another girl, another death.

It never ends.

You'd think some point, some threshold would be crossed. You'd think there'd be a finality to it all, a moment where that sickening hunger quiets, when the urge, the gnawing inside me, finds peace. But it never does. It always return, clawing its way to the surface like a parasite.

I keep telling myself, "The next one, the next kill. It will be the last one. This time, it will be different."

But it's never different. And I know deep down, **it wil never be different.**

So, I kill again, hoping for something that's never coming. Another girl.

And another. And another.

This isn't about power, or sex, or control, not the way they say it is. It's about filling a hole that can never be filled. Something hollow and dark in me that no amount of blood can ever satisfy.
It'll go on until I'm stopped. And even then, there's a part of me that will never be at rest. The endless cycle, a hunger, a void that will stretch beyond this life and maybe the next.

Because no matter how many I kill, **I will never be fulfilled.**

Before each kill, I convince myself, **this is the one**, this is when I finally find it. That moment of peace, of fullness, of silence. But history shows me, it never happens. It never will.

***

Serial Killers and the Hollow Inside

A serial killer is legally defined as a person who commits murder against three or more people. But is it ever just about the number? No. It's about something deeper, something darker. It's about a compulsion that can never be quenched.

Much of what we know about serial killers comes from conversations with men like Ted Bundy. The FBI has built psychological profiles based on their words, their admissions, their confessions of a reality most people can't begin to comprehend. Mental gratification drives most of them, the belief that somehow, in the act of killing, they'll find satisfaction, a release, maybe even redemption.

But that's the cruel irony. **It never happens.**

Serial killers are not just murderers; they are predators, driven by impulses they don't fully understand themselves. The reasons for their killings vary, some kill out of anger, others for the thrill, some for attention. But beneath it all, there's a hollow place, a place they try to fill through death, but it's never enough.

For them, the killings won't stop until they're arrested or killed. Because no matter how many die at their hands, **they will never feel complete.**

***

The Profile of a Killer

A killer doesn't wake up one day and decide to take a life. It builds over time, layer upon layer. Their actions, seemingly without motive, follow a predictable behavior pattern, one that psychologists have come to understand, though never fully explain.

Serial killers often fantasize for years before they ever claim their first victim. These dark thoughts take root, grow, and mutate into obsession. Eventually, they reach a tipping point where fantasy and reality blur, and they cross the line. And once crossed, there's no going back.

The most chilling part? **They don't care.**

Serial killers lack empathy to a degree most of us can't fathom. There's no guilt, no remorse. They see people as objects, mere vessels to satisfy a primal urge. Empathy is a foreign concept, lost somewhere in their twisted psyche, buried beneath layers of trauma, neglect, and deviance.

Their victims aren't people, they're prey. Objects to be used, discarded, and forgotten. Their only value lies in what they represent to the killer: an ideal, a fantasy brought to life. Once that fantasy is played out, they cease to matter.

***

Born or Made? The Eternal Question

The debate rages on: are serial killers born, or are they made? Does the violence stem from nature or nurture?

There's evidence to suggest certain individuals are predisposed to violence, genetic markers, brain abnormalities, and a lack of empathy hardwired into their DNA. For some, it's simply biology at play, a cruel twist of fate encoded in their very genes.

But it's not that simple. Environment matters, too. Trauma, abuse, neglect, they all contribute, shaping a child's mind in ways that can't be undone. A separation from the mother early in life, violent homes, absent fathers, it all leaves scars that never heal, wounds that fester until they manifest in the worst possible ways.

Psychologists, scientists, and researchers have spent decades trying to decode the serial killer's mind, to pinpoint what exactly makes them different from the rest of us. But the truth is, the answer may be both simpler and more complex than we can grasp. Some people are just born broken. And once they start, they can't stop.

The Ideal Victim

Most serial killers have an "ideal" victim, a specific type that fits their twisted fantasies. Race, gender, physical appearance, they all play a role in the selection process. But here's the disturbing part: the killer doesn't care who the person is beyond those superficial traits.

They don't care about their hopes, their dreams, or their life. The victim is just a canvas on which they paint their sick vision. Nothing more, nothing less.

So, the killings go on. The hunt continues. And no matter how many die, the killer will always be empty, hollow, unfulfilled. Because the truth they will never admit to themselves is this:

No amount of death will ever make them feel whole.

For Ted Bundy and others like him, it ends only when they're stopped. But even then, even in their final moments, they will still be chasing something they'll never find. **Fulfillment will always be just out of reach.**

***

Mick had always been meticulous in his plans, every detail calculated with precision. Tonight wasn't any different, but this time, it felt more significant. As he watched Melissa step out of her car, his pulse quickened, not from nerves, but from the cold satisfaction that came with control. She was finally here, walking toward him, completely oblivious to the storm that churned within him.

The house was quiet. Too quiet. His mother was gone for the weekend, as expected. There would be no interruptions. Perfect.

He opened the door just before she knocked, his face breaking into a charming smile. "Hi, Missy," he said, his voice calm, masking the chaos in his mind. She stepped inside, her scent filling the air, something sweet and warm, like innocence dressed in naivety.

Mick's thoughts drifted as he watched her. He imagined what her parents might be doing right now, how clueless they were that their precious daughter was walking into something they could never foresee. He pushed the thought aside, focusing on the task at hand. It wasn't about them. It was about her, and what he needed.

"I told my parents I was out with friends," she said, casually slipping out of her shoes. Her words faded into the background of Mick's mind, like noise in a crowded room. His eyes traced the outline of her figure, her laughter as light as the summer air. She was happy, too happy for his liking. But that would change soon.

Dinner was pleasant enough. They talked about things that didn't matter: college plans, friends, their future. It was all so normal, so ordinary. But beneath it all, Mick was aware of the undercurrent, the silent promises they both knew would unfold later in the evening.

When they moved to the bedroom, the air shifted. Melissa was carefree, trusting, completely at ease. Mick was something else entirely. His movements were smooth and deliberate as he set the mood. He put on the movie, though he couldn't care less about it. Her choice didn't matter. None of it did.

The couch was small, but it didn't matter. They were close, closer than they had been before. The awkwardness of adolescence seemed to evaporate between them, and before long, the kisses came, not the hesitant, playful kind. This was different.

Mick's mind raced as he felt the shift in her body, her trust, her surrender. But as the moments passed, that familiar hollow feeling crept in. He had felt it before, every time. The promise of fulfillment, of satisfaction, dangled just out of reach. His hands moved with purpose, calculated, cold, detaching her from her sense of safety, pulling her closer to the edge.

Yet, as her head tilted back under his grip, the emptiness grew. He'd done this before. It was all the same. There was no satisfaction, no fulfillment. Just the endless cycle of need and disappointment. He would kill her, he knew that much, but he also knew the truth, a truth he had been running from.

It would never be enough. Not her. Not the next girl. Not the one after.

It would go on, just as it always had, just as it always would, until someone stopped him. The question wasn't whether he could fulfill this desire, it was when would the hollow finally consume him completely?

The room was dimly lit by the flickering light from the television, casting dancing shadows across the walls as Mick ran his tongue across Melissa's neck. Her skin was warm, and her breath came in shallow, excited bursts. The atmosphere felt thick, electric, as though the air itself knew what was coming.

"Ooh, you're a little forceful... a little dominant," she whispered, a slow grin spreading across her face, eyes still closed. "I like it."

Mick's hands moved swiftly, almost mechanically, pulling her shirt over her head. Her bra had already slipped from her shoulders, now a forgotten heap in her lap. Melissa, eyes shut, arched her back against the couch, surrendering to the moment as Mick's mouth moved to her breasts, his tongue tracing her nipples. Her left hand traveled down, feeling the hardness that strained against his jeans. This was no innocent game; they were both fully aware of what they wanted.

The only sound, aside from their breathing, was the low murmur of the movie playing on the TV. The room was a private world, sealed off from the rest of existence. His hands slid lower, down her spine, and between her thighs, fingers tracing her body with calculated precision. It was foreplay, but in Mick's mind, it was so much more than that.

He smiled inwardly, knowing this was far from a typical teenage hook-up. They were both 18, no longer naive, no longer questioning desires or inhibitions. This wasn't their first rodeo. But tonight, Mick had something much darker in mind.

As he touched her, Mick's thoughts shifted, dark clouds swirling in his mind. "She's beautiful," he mused. "All she wants is a couple of orgasms, a good time before college... and here I am, planning something else entirely." His thoughts felt disconnected, yet disturbingly clear. "What's wrong with me?" The same question he had asked himself for years, since he was 12, when he first felt the cold thrill of cruelty, when he killed a cat for no reason, and later tortured small animals. He had always chalked it up to some deep, hidden flaw. Or was it something worse?

His hand moved from her chest to her waist, gripping her firmly as he helped her lie down on the couch. Melissa, eyes still closed, let out a soft moan, her arms stretching above her head. Her lips parted, her breath coming in slow, rhythmic sighs. She didn't notice the shift in the air, didn't see the calculation in Mick's eyes as he removed her shorts and panties.

"This feels too easy," Mick thought as he stared at her, exposed and vulnerable before him. But his mind kept circling back, gnawing at him like a parasite. "Am I insane? Or just someone fulfilling a dark fantasy?" His hands twitched, but he didn't stop. He couldn't.

From beneath the couch cushion, Mick pulled out a length of rope. Melissa barely opened her eyes as she noticed it grazing her skin. "Oh my... are you going to get kinky on me, Mick?" she giggled, her voice a lazy whisper. "Okay, be gentle, Master." She turned her head sideways, her hands resting on the arm of the couch, completely trusting him.

He tied her wrists, the ropes taut but not painful. He wanted to savor this. The illusion of control. Melissa lay there, naked, her arms securely bound, as Mick hovered over her, kissing her skin, teasing her body. But his mind was somewhere else entirely. Thoughts of violence, of power, of crossing that final, irreversible line were spiraling through his head like a storm. His father's hunting knife was hidden beneath the couch, waiting. The same knife his father had gifted him years ago, a twisted legacy of the violence he had grown up witnessing.

"Jesus Christ... what the fuck am I?" Mick asked himself, his hands trembling as they moved over her skin. "Am I just playing a role, fulfilling some fantasy, or am I a monster? This is it... the moment where everything changes."

His tongue flicked across her belly, and his hand slid under the couch cushion, retrieving the blade. He held it in both hands, the cold steel resting on his knees as he looked down at her. Melissa's eyes fluttered open. At first, there was no fear. Just confusion.

"Mick... what are you doing?" Her voice cracked, the grin on her face faltering. Her world, once filled with the promise of pleasure, began to shatter as the glint of the knife caught her eye. The playful light in her eyes turned to something primal. Terror.

He didn't respond. He couldn't. The blade hovered above her chest, his fingers gripping the handle tighter than ever before. His breath was shallow, erratic. The first cut was hesitant, sinking just a couple of inches into her flesh, enough to draw blood, but not enough to kill. Melissa's scream pierced the room, sharp and agonizing, but Mick barely heard it. Blood trickled down her chest, pooling near her armpit.

Everything in his mind shifted at once. He had expected satisfaction, some sense of catharsis, but instead, there was only chaos. In the midst of Melissa's panicked breaths, he suddenly heard something else. A faint giggle, barely audible over the TV, and Melissa's sobs.

Mick's head jerked up. The flickering light of the television illuminated the far corner of the room, where a figure stood, small and sharply dressed. A man, wearing a three-piece suit and a bowler hat, with a twisted smile on his face.

"Hello, friend," the figure said, his voice smooth, almost soothing.

Mick's mouth went dry, his heart racing in a way that had nothing to do with the act he had just committed. "You... have got to be fucking kidding me," he whispered, frozen in place.

"Oh no, Mick," the figure replied, tipping his hat slightly. "I'm quite real."

Mick sat there, straddling Melissa, her wrists still bound, her chest heaving as blood trickled from her wound. His mind whirled, trying to make sense of what he was seeing. The figure in the corner didn't belong here; he didn't belong anywhere. And yet, here he was.

"Who are you?" Mick demanded, but deep down, he already knew the answer. He had always known.

The man in the bowler hat smiled wider, the shadows playing tricks with his face. "Why, you know me already... Lucifer at your service."

The weight of the knife in Mick's hand felt heavier now, like a lead weight dragging him into the abyss. And as he stared at the dark figure before him, he realized there was no turning back. This wasn't just a fantasy. It was the beginning of something far darker than he could ever have imagined.

Mick's mind was spinning as he tried to process what was happening. "How the hell did you get in here?" he snapped, his voice shaking. "And who the fuck are you?"

Lucifer, a short man in a three-piece suit, gazed at him with an unsettling calm. "Like I said before... I'm your friend." He looked down at Melissa, who was still struggling to free her wrists from the rope, her breathing shallow and frantic. "I love your work," he said with an eerie grin. "We must ensure it continues. You have a message to send, in your own way."

Mick felt his head swimming. He couldn't make sense of this bizarre situation. The knife still trembled in his hand as he stared at the man before him. "Again...who the fuck are you?"

Lucifer sighed, as though bored by the question. "I'm tired of people asking that," he muttered. "I'm here to understand you. To study your kind." He stepped closer, his fingers brushing Melissa's hair, his smile growing darker. "Poor Melissa," he whispered, his voice like ice. "You know your first victim, but in time, your others won't. That's the key, Mick. You must protect your identity."

Mick's thoughts raced. **This is insane.** "You were hiding here this whole time? You've been in my closet?" His words barely registered as Melissa's desperate voice cut through. "Mick, please let me go... I won't tell anyone. Please. Please!" Her voice was trembling, her wide eyes filled with terror. Lucifer glanced at her with a sneer. "Well, Mick, what's your plan? Let her go? Let her run to the police and tell them about the man who broke into your house? What are you going to do now?" he taunted, his eyes gleaming with cruel amusement.

Mick's grip tightened around the knife. His mind was a whirlwind of confusion and rage. **This isn't how it was supposed to go.** His gaze shifted between the girl beneath him and the strange man who seemed to know everything about him. **Kill them both.**

In a sudden burst of fury, Mick swung the knife at Lucifer's neck, the blade slicing deeply from one side to the other. It was a clean cut, which should have been fatal. But Lucifer didn't flinch. He simply smiled, his hand rising to touch the wound, where no blood flowed. The gash seemed to swallow darkness, and in mere seconds, it sealed itself shut, leaving no trace.

Mick's heart pounded as he stared in disbelief, his hands trembling. "What the hell...?"

Melissa lay frozen, her breath coming in quick, terrified gasps. She, too, had seen the impossible. Lucifer leaned forward, bowing slightly. "I'll forgive you for that, Mick," he said calmly. "Though I'm not entirely sure why. But let's clear things up: I am the Devil."

Mick recoiled. "The fuck you are…"

Lucifer's eyes gleamed. "Think about it, Mick. You nearly decapitated me, and here I stand." His voice was calm, almost cheerful. "I could tell you so many things: names, dates, futures you wouldn't believe. But that's not why I'm here. I'm here because I want to understand your kind. And I already know what you're going to do." He stepped closer, his voice dropping to a sinister whisper. "If you were arrested, and you told the police you saw the Devil, they'd laugh at you. They'd ask you what he was wearing, how tall he was, and they'd think you were insane. You'd end up in a padded cell, talking to me, and no one would believe you."

Lucifer giggled, a chilling, high-pitched sound that echoed in the darkened room. "You see, Mick, they'd lock you away. They'd call you crazy. And I'd still be here, telling you all about the world you'll never see again."

Mick felt a cold sweat break out across his skin. He was trapped, not just in the room, but in his own mind. Melissa's shallow breaths were the only sound now, her body shaking with terror, unable to move or scream. Lucifer leaned in closer, his voice dripping with malevolence.

"And that question you keep asking yourself…why do I do this? It's not just a feeling, Mick. It's in you. It's in your DNA, something that's grown inside you like a cancer. You think this will be enough, but it won't. After Melissa is on the slab, you will crave it again, the need will return, stronger each time. You'll seek out another woman. A new victim."

Lucifer pointed a bony finger at Mick, his laughter rising again, loud and cruel. "You know I'm right, Mick. Once you start, you'll never stop!"

Mick's head spun with a sickening realization. **He's right**. No matter how hard he tried to shake it, the truth settled into his bones. Melissa wasn't just his first; she was the beginning. The darkness inside him wasn't going anywhere. He glanced up at the ceiling, whispering under his breath, "Oh my God..."

Lucifer's grin widened. "I have errands to run," he said casually, like he was leaving a friendly gathering. "But here's my advice: start by burning little Melissa and the couch. Even if you clean it, the blood will still be there. Make your statement clear, Mick. Keep your future victims unaware of who you are. Be smart. Stay away from the police. And remember, our Father watches. He'll know exactly what you've done."

As Mick lowered his eyes back to Melissa, he saw the fear etched across her face. With a single, savage motion, he slashed the blade across her neck, the blood pouring freely. He looked up, expecting to see Lucifer's wicked grin, but the Devil was gone. The room was empty, save for the flickering light from the TV.

Mick stared into the darkness, his mind a haze of confusion and horror. **What the fuck just happened?** he thought, trying to piece together the nightmarish reality.

He drove her car into the garage and waited until the dead of night...3 a.m. When he was sure no one was watching, he burned her body and the couch in the backyard fire pit.

His life had changed forever. He had a new... order.

2

Promises in Blood

Mick stepped out of the tool store into the dim, fading light of the evening. His eyes squinted against the setting sun as he adjusted the brown paper bag in his grip, its weight oddly comforting against his palm. Inside were seemingly harmless items, a map, a few ballpoint pens, a thick, pocket-sized notebook, and a small, cold brass sphere. The sphere, no bigger than four inches across, sat heavily in his hand, the sheen of the polished steel catching the last rays of light. But it wasn't the sphere that held his attention, it was the gnawing thought, the dark presence that had lingered ever since *that night*.

He felt it creeping up again, that *memory*, lurking at the edges of his consciousness. His mind spiraled back to the moment he had finished with Melissa, her body limp under his grasp, the life drained from her eyes. But more unsettling than her death was *him, that thing*, the figure that had appeared out of nowhere. **"I am the Devil,"** the man had said with a quiet confidence that sent a chill through Mick's spine. *Bullshit*, Mick had thought at the time. A delusion. Just another man. But Mick's hand twitched instinctively, recalling the moment his blade had cut through flesh, deep and deliberate. **He had felt the blade slice through the Devil's throat, heard the wet, gurgling sound of severed muscle and trachea.**

And yet, **thirty seconds later**, the man had been whole again. No blood. No wound. Just a ghostly wink, so casual, so eerie that it seemed to burn itself into Mick's memory. **A wink that promised dark things**, a silent message that this was far from over.

He wasn't the kind of man to scare easily; fear had never been an issue for him. But the memory of that wink haunted him in a way that no police or detective could. His first kill had been real, of that he was certain. He had felt the thrill, the intoxicating rush of power that came with taking a life, but this, this figure, *this Devil*, had turned that feeling upside down. The more he thought about it, the more surreal it seemed, like a hallucination that flickered in and out of his mind.

He stepped into his car, the bag of supplies on the passenger seat, and started the engine. It had been months since he'd ended Melissa, months since the newspapers had started running her story, a **10K reward** that had swelled to **50K** for any information leading to her body. The headlines still blared the same message: *Missing. No leads. Family pleads for answers.*

Mick had kept an eye on every article, every whisper from the police, making sure there were no loose threads that could unravel his carefully constructed alibi. He wasn't careless. He was meticulous. He knew they were clever, the detectives, the investigators, sharp enough not to reveal everything they knew to the public. He admired that in a way. **But they were still blind**. No real suspects. No arrests. Just whispers in the dark, and Mick, unseen, continued to move freely among them.

He recalled the way Melissa had casually told her parents she was meeting friends that night. The friends, of course, had told the police the truth; they hadn't seen her in days. Mick smirked at the thought. The police were clueless, chasing shadows.

As he pulled into the driveway of his mother's house, the weight of the day's normalcy crashed down on him like a suffocating blanket. He grabbed the groceries from the back seat, locking the door behind him. Inside, the house smelled faintly of his mother's perfume, the air still warm from the afternoon sun that had filtered through the lace curtains. It felt wrong, almost *too normal* for someone like him to live in a place so mundane. He put the groceries away, his mind miles away from the humdrum of daily life.

His bedroom was small but functional, tucked away from the rest of the house, giving him the privacy he needed. Connected to it was an even smaller room, his sanctuary. A cluttered desk stood against one wall, littered with old photographs, half-empty notebooks, and a series of strange trinkets he had collected over the years, *things that had no real purpose but comforted him in their oddness.* But tonight, his focus was on the map he had laid out across the desk. Towns and cities blurred together under his gaze, each one a potential hunting ground, each one offering the promise of new fulfillment.

But something gnawed at him, *a deep hunger*, an emptiness he couldn't shake. The thrill of killing Melissa had faded like a distant dream. He had been so **infatuated** with the act at first, *elated, fulfilled*, but now? Now it felt like it had never happened. The memory was slipping away, dissolving like fog under the morning sun. **Was it a nightmare? A dream?** The line between reality and imagination was becoming thin, threadbare, as if his mind was actively trying to erase the experience from his memory.

It frightened him, not the killing itself, but the *disappearance* of that moment. He had read about it before, **REM sleep**, how the brain worked in mysterious ways when people dreamed. Tests had shown that those woken up during **rapid eye movement** sleep often remembered their dreams more vividly. But this? This felt like something else. **Dissociation**, a complete erasure of Melissa from his mind, like she had never existed.

His heart raced as he realized it wasn't just Melissa. **It was the feeling**. The satisfaction. The rush of *fulfillment* had vanished too, leaving behind nothing but a hollow ache, a gnawing need that consumed his thoughts. He needed another. Another life. Another thrill. Something to *feed the void* that was growing inside him. It was like a cancer, spreading slowly, quietly, until it consumed everything. He needed his next victim. Soon.

And then there was the Devil. That **man, or whatever he was**. Mick had never forgotten the look in his eyes, the way he had seemed to see right through him, as if he understood every dark desire, every twisted thought that plagued Mick's mind. **That wink**. It was a taunt, a promise, a curse. It was as if the Devil had known, even then, that Mick would end up here, craving more. **"I know you better than you know yourself,"** the Devil had said with that infernal wink, though the words had never left his lips. They didn't need to.

Night fell quickly, and with it came the dream. *Or was it a nightmare?* Mick could never tell anymore. In the dream, he was surrounded by women, beautiful, graceful, but always just out of reach. Each one looked at him, their eyes full of pity, and smiled, a small, tight-lipped smile, just before turning away. It wasn't the outright rejection that hurt, but the subtlety of it. *A rejection masked by politeness*, a smile that said, **"No, but I won't be cruel about it."**

And then, as always, there was the Devil. He stood at the edge of the scene, dressed impeccably in a three-piece suit, a bowler hat perched neatly on his head. Thin and small, he seemed almost unremarkable, but Mick knew better. The Devil wasn't looking at him, not at first. He stood, facing away, watching the women disappear one by one. But when they were all gone, the Devil turned. His eyes gleamed in the darkness, cold and knowing, and he stepped closer to Mick, his voice a low, growling whisper: **"Fire… the angels fell… deep thunder rolled around their shores… burning with the fire of Orc."**

Mick shot awake, the words echoing in his mind. **Angels fell?** Was the Devil speaking about himself? Or was he speaking about Mick?

Breathless, Mick stumbled into the small room, his hands shaking as he pulled the notebook from the drawer. He flipped to the back cover and scrawled the word **"Blonde"**, Melissa's only remaining existence in his world. Then, without hesitation, he unfolded the map, eyes scanning for the next city, the next victim, the next fulfillment. His voice was barely a whisper, but the words came with an edge of desperation: **"I need fulfillment…soon."**

The Devil's wink flashed before his eyes again, taunting him, daring him to take the next step.

3

In The Grip of Desire

The faint morning light filtered through the blinds of Mick Enderson's small room. The space was sparse and functional. He liked it this way, clean and unencumbered. It helped keep his mind focused, though these days, his thoughts were rarely clear. They seemed to spin back to fragments of his past, like a record skipping over the same tracks again and again.

His father. A man he barely remembered. More of a shadow than a person, and the memories Mick did have were hazy at best. He recalled the old farmhouse out in the countryside where his father had worked the land, helping his own parents raise crops and hunt for food when times were lean. His father was a hunter, a serious man who used his hands and his rifle to keep them fed. He'd often taken Mick out with him, teaching him to stalk deer in the early mornings when the frost still clung to the grass. Those hunts were the only real bond they shared, and even then, there had been an unsettling quiet between them.

Mick had never known his biological father. The man had disappeared from his life long before Mick could even ask questions. He had vague recollections, his parents' stony silence, their refusal to speak of certain things, yet never openly arguing. His mother, Sara, always disagreed with his father in subtle ways, but she had a way of never letting those disagreements escalate into confrontation. Now, with his father long dead and no family farm left to inherit, Mick realized how little had actually passed down to him. The farm had been sold off years ago, and whatever meager insurance might have existed vanished along with his father's last job.

The only one who had truly taken care of him was his mother. She'd seen the absence of a financial safety net and acted swiftly, buying herself a solid life insurance policy. When she passed, Mick would be taken care of, if not out of love, then out of practicality. That was how Sara always was, practical to a fault. But Mick wasn't concerned about money. His thoughts were preoccupied by something else, something deeper and darker.

Mick had to figure out his next move. He wanted to continue his education, not out of any desire to see himself thrive, but because he believed it was necessary. For Mick, education was simply a means to an end. Dunwood Technical College, located only ten miles away, seemed like the easiest choice. It was close, affordable, and offered programs that were practical enough to satisfy himself. It wasn't that Mick cared about construction or management; it was simply a path to follow, a way to keep moving without standing out too much.

***

The next morning, he drove to the campus. Dunwood's campus was as unremarkable as he expected, red-brick buildings spread out across the grounds, students milling about, their faces blurred in the bright morning light.

Inside, he was greeted by Kim, the supervisor of admissions. She was striking, a redhead with sharp, intelligent eyes and a body that immediately caught Mick's attention. She wore a grey pantsuit, well-fitted and professional, but Mick noticed the subtle way it clung to her hips and chest. As she led him through the hallways, showing him the classrooms and labs, her voice was calm, confident, and professional. But Mick wasn't really listening. He was watching her…closely.

"We're very proud of our programs here at Dunwood," Kim said, leading him into her office. "You can start with a two-year program, and if you decide to go further, we offer three-year tracks for more advanced certifications."

Mick nodded, his gaze lingering on her. "I'll start with the two-year degree. It's practical, and I can always move up later, right?"

"Yes, exactly," Kim replied, her smile polite, but Mick could sense a warmth in it that piqued his interest.

As she handed him the paperwork to fill out, Mick struggled to focus. His mother had given him all the necessary details, tuition payments, deadlines, and financial aid. But that wasn't what was on his mind. He watched Kim as she leaned forward slightly, the scent of her perfume, a soft, floral fragrance, filling the small office. His thoughts started to wander. Fantasies began to play out in his mind, vivid and tangible. He imagined what it would be like to be alone with her, just the two of them, with no one to interrupt. Fantasy was one thing, but desire, that was something else entirely. Desire was real, something he could feel building inside him, a pressure he had learned to control. For now, anyway. He knew the difference between wanting and acting. The time would come for action, but not yet.

Kim's voice pulled him back to reality. "We'll just need your signature here, and then we can get you all set up for the first semester," she said, her tone all business.

Mick nodded, signing the forms with a steady hand, though inside, his thoughts were anything but steady. The flicker of fantasies danced behind his eyes, and he had to suppress the urge to smile. She had no idea what went through his mind, how close he was to losing control.

"Thank you, Mick. I think you'll find Dunwood to be a good fit," Kim said, standing up and offering him a firm handshake.

"No, thank you," Mick replied, his voice low, his smile tight. "I think I'll enjoy it here."

As he left the office, his footsteps echoed in the quiet hallways. He could feel the tension inside him, coiling tighter with every step. Outside, the sun had dipped lower in the sky, casting long shadows across the parking lot. Mick watched the students pass by, their conversations muted and distant. They had no idea who he really was, what thoughts swirled in his mind. But that was fine, he liked it that way.

He slid into the driver's seat of his car, staring out at the campus as dusk began to settle. The voice in the back of his head reminded him to be patient. *Hide your desires. Don't make it easy for them to find you. Be careful, be deliberate.*

***

The weekend would come soon enough, and with it, the chance to release the tension building inside him. But for now, he would wait. He had always been good at waiting, and when the time came, he would be ready. The mask of normalcy fit him well; he just had to keep it in place a little longer.

That night, Mick sat at his computer for hours, his mind whirling like the whir of the hard drive. The dim light of the screen flickered across his face as he scrolled mindlessly through YouTube videos: music, sports, maps of places long forgotten. His fingers danced on the keys, but his thoughts were elsewhere, slipping into darker corners of his mind. The fantasies crept in, unbidden, swirling in his imagination like a storm. He leaned back in his chair, eyes half-closed, and whispered into the empty room, *Is there a way to take care of my desires without breaking man's laws?*

It seemed impossible. The tension between impulse and consequence, fantasy and law, always pulled him in opposite directions. *No reflection of my desires, he thought bitterly, without crossing the line.*

His eyes flicked to the small notebook lying next to his keyboard. It was plain, unassuming, the kind of thing someone might use for grocery lists or reminders. But Mick had other uses for it. Flipping it open, he saw the single word, *blonde*, scrawled in sharp, deliberate letters next to a name: Melissa. He'd thought, for a brief moment, about keeping a souvenir from her, something tangible, a lock of hair, a trinket from her purse. But that would have been reckless, leaving behind something so incriminating. Instead, he settled on writing down the color of her hair. Just that. Detached, impersonal, as if it reduced her to something less than human. Her name? It hardly mattered. The only thing that would remind him of his victims now was what he found in their wallets or purses. Their names were irrelevant, just another detail to erase.

He rubbed a hand across his face and muttered to himself, "I'll never forget that piece of shit who showed up when Melissa died. That bastard knows more about my future than I do. He'll be with me until the end."

The memory of that night gnawed at him like a splinter buried deep under the skin. He could still see it, the figure who had appeared out of nowhere, who had *seen him*. And yet, something about it wasn't right. It was too dark to make out much, but Mick remembered one thing with chilling clarity: the man hadn't bled. The knife had sliced clean through his throat, but no blood came. Instead, the wound had sealed itself, black and twisted, as if the skin were made of something otherworldly. And the man had *smiled* at him. Smiled and *winked* as the flesh knitted back together, as if he was amused by Mick's confusion. It had shaken Mick more than he cared to admit. Was that man even human? He couldn't be. But what was he?

Mick shook his head, trying to push the thoughts away. There was no room for hesitation. He brought up maps on his computer again, scanning for potential hunting grounds. His eyes locked onto a familiar name: *Tawn City.* A small community thirty miles out, where Mick had played baseball as a kid. He remembered it vividly, the dusty diamonds, the Burger Shack where they used to eat lunch after games, and the Bar & Grill next to it.

It was the perfect spot. The entrance was wide, and a row of thick bushes ran alongside the sidewalk, offering plenty of cover. Women, young, carefree, probably drunk, would come to places like this for a night out. Most of them were with friends, but there would always be a few stragglers. A few who were alone.

He could see it all in his mind's eye. Black clothes, blending into the shadows. The bushes concealing him until the perfect moment. He smiled to himself, a cold, calculated smile. *Ideal.*

He leaned back in his chair, recalling a line from an old movie that had stuck with him. "Every time you commit a crime, there are fifty ways you can fuck up, and you'll only think of ten of them," the character had said. Mick smirked. *Yeah, I'll probably fuck up. But that's just part of the game.*

He grabbed a paper map from his desk, circling Tawn City in red ink. "This weekend," he whispered.

***

The week flew by, everything falling into place as Mick got ready for Tech College. Friday came quicker than he thought it would, and with it, the surge of excitement he'd been holding back. Mick's car was loaded, everything he'd need packed neatly. At night, he'd wear black, disappearing into the darkness. During the day, he'd blend in with the normal crowd, just another face passing by. The plan was simple: head down Friday, watch, wait, memorize how people moved in and out of the bar and grill. Then Saturday, he'd find her, the one who would finally quench the burning inside him. By late Saturday, he'd be back home, like nothing ever happened.

In the trunk, Mick kept his tools, an iron ball, three inches wide, perfect for knocking someone out cold. Rope. Handcuffs. Everything was ready. There'd be no hotel, too risky. He'd sleep in the car, out of sight, invisible.

Just some food, water, and a change of clothes. Nothing that could be traced back to him.

But Mick couldn't shake the thought of *him*, the one who saw it all when he killed Melissa. It's impossible to forget. Was he wearing something over his neck, something plastic? The night had been dark, sure, but not that dark. He remembered the knife slicing through him, clear as day. he was only two feet away. The trachea wide open, split clean. He felt the blade hit, heard it. But no blood, just blackness. And the way he smiled as it... healed itself? It made no sense. Was he even human? Was that the Devil? The thought still gnaws at him.

Mick pushed it away as he drove, the gas tank full, heading into Tawn City. The baseball diamonds came into view, and for a second, he remembered playing there as a kid. The Walmart just beyond them would be his stop for the night, a perfect hiding spot. No one would think twice about a car parked there overnight.

When Mick got to the bar, he parked at a distance, just far enough to see everything but not be seen. The thick bushes by the sidewalk were ideal cover. People came and went in pairs or small groups, sometimes alone. Mick had his binoculars, small, expensive, but they did the job. He could see everything.

The night came alive around me as the sun sank and the weekend crowd filled the place. Mick sat there, calm, eating his turkey sandwich, sipping Coke, watching. The doors swung open and shut in a steady rhythm. Two minutes, five, maybe ten between each person. That was all he needed. Mick could be in and out in less than 20 seconds, 15 if he was fast. He pictured it: the iron ball striking her skull, her body collapsing, then dragging her into the back seat. So simple. It would be over before anyone knew what had happened.

When he'd seen enough, Mick started the car and headed back to the Walmart lot, pulling into the farthest corner. It was quiet there, safe. He fell asleep easily, knowing that tomorrow everything would go as planned.

Saturday arrived without a hitch. Mick parked on the other side of the bushes, where a smaller lot served the office building next to the bar. Drinkers often parked there. It had three handicapped spaces, and he took the closest one, using a fake "van accessible" sign. Around him, the lot was mostly empty, a few cars here and there. Mick checked for cameras. Nothing. He smiled. Perfect.

He stepped out, dressed in dark jeans and a long black smock, blending into the night. His car doors were unlocked, the iron ball heavy in his hand, ready. Mick crouched in the bushes, his heart steady, his mind racing through every detail. Thirty miles from home, everything had to be flawless. Tonight, he'd do it. No doubt. No hesitation. It was all set in motion.

Mick crouched in the darkness, my legs numb from kneeling, but he didn't care. The anticipation was a sick thrill, crawling through him like a cold serpent. For almost an hour, he watched people shuffle in and out of the bar, like puppets on strings, unaware of the eyes lurking behind the thick bushes. It reminded Mick of *The Tell-Tale Heart*, that constant pounding beneath the surface. He stifled a giggle, the sound barely escaping his lips, as a drunk guy stumbled after his girlfriend, begging her to stop. A lovers' quarrel. They always thought they were the center of the universe, so unaware of what really lurked in the shadows.

Mick was hidden well, tucked behind the thick leaves, far from the light. The entrance glowed with a sickly hue, but it didn't reach him. He felt invisible, like the madman in Poe's story, watching with the intensity of that vulture's eye. No one could see him here. Mick was the predator, waiting. He could feel the sweat building under his clothes, mixing with the cool night air as his eyes scanned the crowd for *her*, the one he'd take.

The crowd varied, a parade of people lost in their weekend haze, none of them suspecting the danger waiting just outside their reality. Mick had been patient for over an hour when the moment finally arrived. A woman stepped out of the bar, standing there under the dim streetlight. She was alone. Perfect. She fiddled with her phone, her fingers tapping out a message while her eyes flickered up and down the street. No one was coming or going. The street was dead.

He felt a surge of adrenaline, his pulse hammering in his ears. This was it. Everything lined up so perfectly, no witnesses, no distractions. His heart quickened as he watched her, a slim brunette in her mid-twenties, maybe early thirties. She was just the right size, just the right type. She slipped her phone into her purse and began to walk.

Time stretched unbearably thin. It felt like hours for her to pass where Mick was hidden, though it was only seconds. He could hear his breath in his ears, feel the heat of his own blood coursing through his veins as she got closer. When she was just feet away, Mick scanned the sidewalk, the parking lot. Nothing. Not a single movement.

It was time.

He rose from my crouch, moving silently, a predator in the night. Every step felt too loud, though he knew he was silent. Then, the snap of a twig beneath his foot. Her head whipped around, eyes wide, just as he swung the iron ball.

The sickening thud of metal meeting bone echoed in the still air. She crumpled instantly, her knees hitting the pavement with a muted thud. No scream, no time for her to react. Mick lunged forward, wrapping his arm around her chest, clamping a hand over her mouth before any sound could escape. Her body was limp, her breath shallow, as he dragged her through the bushes, heart pounding in his chest.

Mick glanced around, paranoid, every shadow feeling like it might move. But no one was there. No figures, no footsteps, nothing. The world felt utterly still as he hauled her toward his car, her body sagging against his.

It only took a few more moments to shove her into the backseat, her limbs limp but starting to twitch. A low moan escaped her lips. Mick gritted his teeth and brought the iron ball down on her again, softer this time, just enough to quiet her. Her moaning stopped.

Quickly, he cuffed her hands behind her back and wrapped a rope tightly around her ankles. The blanket went over her body, hiding her from view, just another lump in the backseat of an ordinary car.

Mick slid into the driver's seat, his hands trembling with the thrill of it all. As he pulled onto the highway, the car felt unnervingly quiet, save for the occasional low grunt from the backseat. As Mick glanced into the rearview mirror, a glint of something caught his eye. Her purse, half-spilled onto the floorboard, had slid open during the scuffle. Curiosity tugged at him, and with one hand on the wheel, he reached back and rummaged through the mess. His fingers landed on her wallet, flipping it open. There it was, her ID card. Evelyn. Her name was Evelyn. Something about knowing her name made it all the more real. He tossed the wallet aside, his knuckles tightening on the steering wheel.

Mick kept driving, his mind racing, replaying the scene over and over.

She was mine now. And no one would ever know.

4

The Devil's Ruminations

The Devil leaned back, a flicker of amusement curling at the edges of his darkened thoughts as he gazed at Priest Brown. A man who was a paradox, woven from threads of faith, compassion, and a peculiar curiosity for the darker recesses of the human mind. The Devil had watched him closely for years, admired the contradictions within him, the kind that so often pulled men into his clutches. For Priest Brown, life was a delicate balance between faith and intellect, between the intangible spirit and the hardened facts of psychology.

Yes, Priest Brown was fascinating. But what truly captivated the Devil's attention was the knowledge that Mick's path would soon intersect with this man. It was not a vision of the future; he could not see the future. No, it was more of a knowing, a familiarity with the undercurrents of human lives and the way certain events inevitably folded into one another like pieces of a puzzle. He could sense how these oddities would align, twisting fate into something wickedly inevitable.

What would the good priest think of Mick? The Devil pondered this with dark delight. Would he dissect Mick's violence through the sterile lens of psychology, labeling it as mere mental illness or some unresolved trauma? Or would he reach for his Bible, muttering verses about sin and redemption, seeing Mick as the embodiment of pure evil, the Devil's own work? *Both are accurate*, the Devil mused, a bitter laugh escaping him.

But it didn't matter how Priest Brown interpreted it. He would not stop the storm that was coming. No one could.

Then there was Andrew Taylor, the detective, another man whose life would inevitably intertwine with Mick's. Taylor was different from Priest Brown. His mind was not clouded by faith or compassion. Taylor was clear-headed, ruthlessly logical, driven by the singular goal of justice. He had clawed his way up from being a simple patrol officer to homicide, and he had earned every inch of that climb. The Devil couldn't help but admire him. There was something satisfying about the way men like Taylor threw themselves into their work, following every clue, piecing together the fragments of human misery, and yet, in the end, justice often eluded them.

Poor Taylor, the Devil thought. He would meet Mick soon, and while the details of that meeting remained obscure, the Devil knew the outcome would be deliciously messy. Justice, for all its pretensions, was fickle at best. Taylor would chase the truth, but he would never grasp it, not fully. Mick was not a mere criminal; he was something older, more primal, a manifestation of the chaos embedded in human nature. The Devil almost pitied Taylor. Almost.

The Devil turned his attention inward, to the ancient truth that had guided his existence for millennia. He had been called many names over the ages: Diablos, Satan, Lucifer. Some saw him as an accuser, a slanderer. Others blamed him for every catastrophe, every war, every act of human depravity. And perhaps they were right to do so. He had sown his share of chaos. But the Devil knew something far more sinister: humans had always carried the seeds of their own destruction within them. They had never needed his help to ruin themselves.

He had been there, watching, for thousands of years. He had seen civilizations rise and fall, empires crumble, and through it all, humans had remained the same, fragile, violent, desperate. The Devil smiled as he thought of the ancient tribes, the way they had once needed men like Mick. Back then, the "Lonely Hunters" were celebrated, necessary even. They were the ones who stalked the wild beasts, who brought food to the tribe, who ensured survival in a savage, unforgiving world. They were brutal, merciless, but they were heroes.

But the world had changed. Humanity had evolved, or so they liked to believe. The Lonely Hunter, once vital, had become a pariah, a twisted remnant of an age long past. What had once been a genetic gift, a survival mechanism honed over millennia, had become a curse. These men, these killers, were no longer necessary for the survival of the species. They were aberrations, glitches in the system, and society hunted them down like animals.

The Devil reveled in this irony. The very trait that had once kept humans alive was now the thing that damned them. The world no longer had use for men like Mick. He was the product of a misfiring gene, an evolutionary artifact that had outlived its purpose. The Devil had seen it countless times, this slow, cruel metamorphosis that had turned humanity into something weaker, something safer. The Lonely Hunters had been bred out, replaced by timid creatures who clung to order and law.

But every so often, the gene would reemerge, a flicker of the old savagery lurking beneath the surface. Men like Mick carried that legacy. They were relics of a time when survival depended on brutality, when heroes were the ones who could kill without remorse. Now, they were monsters, and society had no place for them.

Mick didn't know it, but the Devil did. He had seen it all before. This "unbalanced" gene that modern man so feared, this predisposition to violence, was nothing more than nature's way of remembering. Humanity, in all its arrogance, thought it had moved beyond such things, but the Devil knew better. Evolution had no regard for morality. It did not care for law or justice. It only cared for survival, and sometimes, survival required a monster.

Mick was that monster, the embodiment of an ancient force that humanity had tried to bury. And soon, the world would see him for what he truly was. They would label him a psychopath, a killer, but the Devil knew the truth: Mick was simply a man out of time, a man born with a legacy of violence that no longer fit in the civilized world.

The Devil's smile grew darker. He had always known this about humanity. For all their self-righteousness, for all their talk of progress, they were still animals at heart. Strip away their rules, their laws, their pretenses, and what was left was the same savage creature that had once hunted in the dark.

Priest Brown and Andrew Taylor might try to understand Mick, to rationalize his actions, but they would never truly grasp the depths of it. They would never see that Mick was not a product of evil, but of evolution. He was the inevitable result of a process that had been set in motion long before their precious societies had ever existed.

And the Devil... well, he would be there to watch it unfold, just as he always had. He had no need to intervene, no need to push or prod. Humanity, in its flawed brilliance, would destroy itself. All he had to do was wait.

The Devil leaned back, content. Mick's story was far from over, and as it played out, the Devil would be there, lurking in the shadows, watching with the same amused detachment he had held for millennia.

The Lonely Hunter had returned. And soon, the world would remember why men like him were once necessary.

5

Shadows in the Corner

The room was cloaked in darkness, save for a solitary light flickering in the corner, casting long, wavering shadows that danced menacingly across the cramped space. The air was thick with a pungent odor, reminiscent of decay and desperation, infiltrating every nook and cranny of Mick's confined sanctuary. As he sat hunched in his "boss chair," the small room seemed to breathe and expand around him, the walls inching outward as if closing in on his spiraling thoughts.

Mick stared blankly at the computer screen before him, its harsh glow barely cutting through the oppressive gloom. The light from the corner lamp threw eerie silhouettes that twisted and contorted, mirroring the chaos within his mind. "Why do I do this?" he muttered, the question echoing off the walls, unanswered. He had pondered this countless times, delving into the darkest corners of psychological theory, reading about the motives that plagued the minds of those like him. It wasn't just the motives, though, no, it was something deeper, more insidious. A lack of conscience, a psychopathic personality disorder, an unquenchable need for control, predatory behavior, and an absence of remorse or guilt.

He had immersed himself in research, scouring articles and case studies about serial killers. They spoke of childhood improvisations, of internal forces dictated by DNA, of a dismembered clique where changing a chromosome could unleash a dormant predator. "It's in your DNA," they wrote. "Your environment will bring it out." Mick had clung to those words, trying to rationalize his actions, to find solace in the idea that his tendencies were not entirely his own, but a biological inevitability triggered by his surroundings.

Mick leaned back, his mind a whirlwind of self-examination. "Two killings," he thought, "by proximity, I'm not a serial killer yet. It takes three to register as one." But deep down, he knew he would never stop. This wasn't a choice; it was a disease, a cancer that gnawed at his soul, impossible to eradicate. The fulfillment he felt after taking lives was undeniable. After Melissa and Evelyn's deaths, he had been exhilarated, stimulated, delighted, animated, fueled, intoxicated, and utterly fulfilled. In those moments, he had never felt more alive than at the sight of another person's demise.

He yearned for answers, desperate to understand what coursed through his mind, what drove him to commit these heinous acts. Dominance, control, command, these were his obsessions. He needed his victims to know who was in charge, to feel the overwhelming power he wielded. Their bodies had become his toys, their physical selves owned and manipulated by his will. Melissa had known this, had understood his need for dominance, but Evelyn hadn't. She had been too stunned, too unprepared when he delivered the slickness of his work, the slab of his butchery.

Memories of Melissa lingered sharply in his mind. They had been close to consummating their relationship before something had intervened. Evelyn, on the other hand, had been practically brain-dead by the time he returned to his place. He had dissected her methodically, the process taking hours as he meticulously cleaned up the evidence. He had wanted sex with both women, a twisted desire that never came to fruition, but instead manifested in their deaths.

Mick's thoughts drifted to his mother, the one constant in his fractured life, and the death of his father, a distant memory barely etched into his consciousness. His mother had always been there for him, the pillar he leaned on during his childhood, a time when his father was a stranger. "Mother always matters the most," she had said, her voice firm and commanding, "You will do as I say." She had been his anchor, especially during the darkest times. Punishments for bedwetting extended into his early school years, instilling a fear that lingered long after the physical reprimands ceased. Those memories festered, intertwining with his present actions, shaping his twisted sense of right and wrong.

Dreams haunted him too, dreams where women rejected him, where he stood alone against a backdrop of cold indifference, and the only other presence was Lucifer, watching with an unsettling smile. These dreams were odd, strange, and yet felt like broken pieces of a puzzle he couldn't quite solve. An answer was there, lurking just beyond his grasp, but he never quite managed to piece it together.

He reminded himself of his religious beliefs, grappling with the abstract concepts of Good and Evil. To him, Evil was profoundly immoral and wicked, the primary cause of all that was unwelcome and disagreeable in man's nature. Good, on the other hand, meant helping in a positive way, enhancing the "quality of life." Yet, here he was, embodying the very definition of Evil, orchestrating chaos and destruction under the guise of his twisted sense of purpose.

"I never grew up differently than anyone else," Mick thought, a self-assurance that quickly dissolved under scrutiny. He knew that thought was wrong. Judging oneself was ordinary, but judging oneself accurately? That was indictable and incorrect. He continued his internal monologue, convincing himself that it had to be more related to his DNA. "There is something in there that is completely fucked up," he mused, a bitter acceptance settling over him.

He closed his eyes, hands pressed against each side of his head, trying to block out the increasing stench of cat piss that now filled the room. "How can I not believe in God when I had the Devil witnessing the homicide of Melissa?" he pondered. The slicing of her throat, the clear, open divide across her trachea, every detail vivid and undimmed in his mind. "Then he... cured, and kept telling me that this killing is my future. He had known it all along."

Mick shook his head, his eyes still closed, sitting in his "boss chair" in front of his computer, the corner light still casting its shadowy veil over everything. Beside him, on the ottoman, lay Evelyn's head, one eye shut and the other half-open, the ripe smell overpowering his senses. He couldn't shake the thought that the Devil had given him countless pointers on avoiding the police, insisting he would never keep trophies from his kills. Yet here he was, with Evelyn's head still there, staring back at him.

"Will have to burn the head and after the fire, hammer the skull to pieces," he thought, the plan forming clearly in his mind. He closed his eyes again, never noticing the man standing in the corner until the presence was undeniable. It was St. Lucifer, a shadowy figure observing silently. "One of his favorites," Mick acknowledged internally, a small smile tugging at his lips. Lucifer didn't need to guide him; his actions were already written in his DNA, set in motion by time and circumstance. "I admire him yet feel sorry for him... pity... pity little Mick," Lucifer murmured before disappearing into the darkness, leaving behind a room filled with shadows and the lingering stench of decay.

Mick stood up, glancing down at Evelyn's head one last time. The towel he draped over her face was a small mercy, a final act of control over the chaos he had unleashed. He moved towards the backyard pit, the door creaking open to reveal the cold night air. The darkness outside was almost soothing, a blank canvas for his next act. As he walked away from the room, the shadows seemed to follow, the smell fading slightly but still persistent, a reminder of the lives he had taken and the path he was destined to follow.

He glanced back once more, ensuring there was nothing left to see, then stepped into the night, the weight of his actions pressing down on him as he prepared to continue his twisted journey. The pit awaited, a silent witness to his deeds, and Mick knew that this was just the beginning. The cycle would continue, driven by his need for control, his twisted sense of fulfillment, and the dark forces that whispered in the corners of his mind.

As he began the process of burning away the evidence, the flickering light from the room behind him cast one final shadow, shedding a light on the darkness that consumed him.

6

The Thin Line Between
Shadows and Desire

Months had slipped away since Evelyn's death, the days blurring together as Mick's mind constantly sought distractions. Yet, his routine never changed. Each evening, he diligently sat in front of the TV, watching the six o'clock news or thumbing through the local newspaper. He wasn't one for grand gestures of grief. Instead, he let the numbness guide his days, hoping that the world would forget Evelyn as easily as it had Melissa Miller.

Melissa's disappearance had set the town alight. Posters plastered every lamppost, social media campaigns, and reward money that seemed to grow by the week. She had the kind of parents who knew how to pull strings, influential in ways Mick imagined Evelyn's family never could have been. Evelyn's case had been relegated to a back corner of people's minds, just another missing girl, another unsolved mystery. There was no reward for her. No desperate parents on TV begging for her return. Her death, though it lay heavy on Mick's conscience, didn't weigh on the town's collective memory in the same way.

"Melissa's got the money, the attention, the connections," Mick mused one evening, absently flipping through the newspaper, eyes glazing over the headlines. "Evelyn... she was just another girl in the missing category. No one cared enough to put up money for her."

Yet, beneath the surface of those seemingly indifferent thoughts, something stirred in Mick. His mind often wandered back to Evelyn, not with guilt or sorrow, but with a sense of longing, a hunger for something more. It was an urge he tried to suppress but couldn't ignore, and each passing day only seemed to magnify it.

For Mick, Dunwood College was the only real escape. The campus offered a sanctuary, where the walls of classrooms held his mind hostage, shielding him from the darkness that clawed at his thoughts. Learning provided him with a temporary relief, a mental key to lock away his darker urges. With each new lecture, the world outside felt distant, and he could almost forget who he was or what he had done.

As the years passed, however, his relationship with his mother had withered like a plant neglected in the dark. They still shared the same house, but the bond between them had eroded long ago. His mother, once vibrant and full of life, spent her days with friends or taking trips to hospitals and clinics for cancer treatments. Her years of smoking had finally caught up with her, leaving her body riddled with disease. Mick never asked about her health. He knew the trips were becoming more frequent, the doctor's appointments more urgent. Yet, he was indifferent. His mother had sold the family farm years ago, acres of land, gone in an instant, and Mick suspected she was hiding the money. But he never cared enough to ask. Dunwood was being paid for, and that was enough.

There was only one thing that disrupted his otherwise methodical existence at Dunwood: Kim. She was a redhead with legs that seemed to go on forever, a beauty that sparked something dangerous inside him. His feelings toward her were more than an innocent crush, far darker than mere infatuation. She was a temptation, a challenge, a craving he couldn't quite control.

One evening, as Mick prepared to leave campus, throwing his bag into the back seat of his car, a familiar voice called out to him.

"Hi, Mick!"

He looked up, and there she was, Kim, standing beside her car, her hair catching the last golden rays of the setting sun.

"Kim," Mick responded, his heart racing, though his face remained calm. "How are you doing?"

"I'm good. I hope you're enjoying your time here. Are you getting along with the instructors?" she asked with a smile, oblivious to the intensity of his gaze.

"They're knowledgeable. They give good lectures... and tricks," Mick replied, his words flat, mechanical, masking the hunger brewing inside him.

"Great! If you need anything, don't hesitate to ask," Kim said, turning toward the building.

"Take it easy," Mick managed, but his mind had already drifted into darker places.

As Kim walked up the steps to the main building, Mick felt his pulse quicken. He watched her, his thoughts cold and calculated. Lack of empathy. No guilt. No remorse. These were the words that floated in his mind, drifting in like dark clouds on the horizon. He thought, *I can be superficially charming, luring people into my web without them realizing. But I must be careful. No incidents here. I can't afford to give detectives anything to work with. I have to keep low, bide my time.*

The word "fulfillment" echoed in his mind as Kim disappeared through the doors. It had been so long since Evelyn's death. The hunger was growing again, gnawing at his insides like a beast demanding to be fed. Before Kim vanished, Mick quickly pulled out his phone and snapped a picture of her, catching her just as she entered the building, her long legs a blur as she walked away.

When he got home later that evening, his mother was sitting at the kitchen table. The thought crossed his mind again, whether she was hiding money from the farm sale, but he quickly pushed it aside. It didn't matter.

"How are classes going, Mick?" she asked, her voice strained as though talking had become an effort.

"They're fine," he replied. "I like it there. It's a good place for me."

"That's good to hear," she said, though her tone lacked real interest. She was too consumed by her own world of hospital visits and medical treatments. "There are a lot of girls at Dunwood. Have you asked any of them out?"

Mick forced a smile, though inside, he recoiled at the thought of revealing the truth. *She can't know. She can never know what I really am.*

"There are some nice girls there, but I haven't asked anyone out yet," he lied easily, the smile never leaving his face.

His mother sighed, disappointed. "Well, keep that smile. You'll find someone eventually."

Mick nodded, but his mind was already elsewhere. The mask he wore for his mother, for the world, was paper-thin. Behind it, his desires churned, growing darker with each passing day.

"You've been going to the hospital a lot lately. Is there something I should know?" Mick asked, not out of concern but curiosity. He had never really cared about his mother's health.

"They think it's lung cancer," she said softly, the weight of the words hanging in the air. "Chemotherapy, radiation... it's serious, Mick. But don't worry. I'll be okay."

Mick shrugged. "I'm hungry, Mom. Want to go out to eat?"

"No," she replied, "I'm meeting Sheila and Tara for supper. After that, we're going out for drinks."

"Alright, have a good time," Mick said, his voice neutral, disinterested.

Once his mother left, Mick fired up the grill, throwing on a couple of frozen hamburger patties. As they cooked, his thoughts drifted to Kim, to the photo on his phone, to the growing hunger inside him. *Time is killing me again. Fulfillment is dead*, he thought, the craving intensifying. *The need, the inclination, the craving for my fulfillment is swelling.* He pulled out his phone and stared at the picture of Kim, her figure captured in mid-step, walking up the stairs.

Later that evening, after eating his burgers, he sat down in front of his computer, the darkness of the room enveloping him. He had been planning something for weeks, but tonight, the urge felt overpowering. He opened the map on his screen, scrolling through rest stop areas along highways 63 and 12. They were isolated stretches, with miles of empty road between towns, perfect places for people to stop, perfect places to find someone alone.

His eyes flicked back to the picture of Kim, and he felt the familiar, unsettling thrill return. There were rest stops he remembered from his travels, places he had driven by dozens of times. Some were secluded, out of the way, with just a few cars at any given moment. He would take a trip this weekend, he decided. He'd drive 140 miles up and back, stopping at every rest stop along the way, surveying the area, searching.

There had to be a woman, close to being alone.

The hunger was too much now. It had been too long since Evelyn's death. Too long since the last time his need was satisfied.

This weekend, he would act again.

And this time, he wouldn't wait as long.

7

The Hunter's Vigil

The devil was in his dream again. Mick recognized him immediately, short, clad in a dark suit, bowler hat tilted slightly, and that ever-present sharp, thin mustache. His face, devoid of expression, was a mask of eerie calm. There were no words, just the sea crashing beside him. The wind whipped through the dark, stormy clouds overhead, churning the waters violently as if nature itself responded to the presence of this figure. On the other side of the beach loomed mountains, their jagged peaks disappearing into the mist like some forgotten, haunted land. Mick stood still, the salt in the air stinging his nose, his legs heavy as if rooted to the ground.

The devil, no more than a silhouette against the turbulent backdrop, did his usual contrivance, winked, smiled, and pointed down the shore. It was subtle but chilling. Mick felt a sickening churn in his gut. He knew what was coming, had seen it too many times. His body moved of its own accord, obeying some unseen force. Reluctantly, he turned his gaze to the horizon, toward the women. Two figures, backs to him, motionless at the edge of the shoreline.

"Shit," Mick whispered, the dream unraveling. His eyes snapped open, tearing him from the nightmare into the dim reality of his room. Sweat clung to his skin, soaking his sheets. He sat up in bed, head in his hands, trying to calm the pounding in his chest. The dream wasn't just a dream; it never was. The devil's grin, the wink, the women on the shore. They all meant something. And deep down, he knew what it was. It always came back to Melissa.

The night she died, he had seen him, the devil, in the flesh. Mick had been there, the knife in his hand, the blood on the floor, and yet, impossibly, the man he sliced open stood there with that same insidious smile. No magic tricks, no escape artist games, just a deep, clean cut and a knowing grin. The devil never spoke, but his presence said enough. There was no escaping it now.

Morning light crept through the blinds as Mick swung his legs off the bed, his mind a haze of confusion and guilt. He replayed last night, filling up his car, preparing for something, but what? It didn't matter. "No way out of this situation," he muttered to himself. Life had become a blur of days blending into each other, a cycle of survival in a world that made less and less sense. But there were moments, brief flashes of clarity, where his true desires reared their head. His mind would burn with ambition, with lust for control, for power, for domination.

The mirror reflected a stranger. Mick stared at his own face, calm, cold, detached. But behind the eyes, there was a storm brewing. He showered mechanically, barely registering the water against his skin. When he came downstairs, the house was silent. Mom wasn't there. She rarely was these days. Cancer had ravaged her body, and with it, any hope of the relationship they once had. He didn't ask questions anymore; he didn't care.

The morning passed in a blur at Dunwood's library. He didn't care for the mundane lives of the other students, their quiet dedication to grades and careers. He was drawn to darker things, the forbidden sections of knowledge. Books on murder, evil, and unspeakable acts. He thumbed through pages detailing violence, bloodshed, and wickedness, all while his peers remained blissfully unaware. The library was his haven, his secret escape, a sanctuary for the twisted thoughts that festered in his mind.

Hours passed, the afternoon slipping away as he gathered everything he needed, not books, not notes, but images, knowledge, pieces of the puzzle in his head. By the time he returned home, dusk had begun to fall. Mom's car was in the driveway, and the house was still eerily quiet. He pushed open her door and found her asleep, snoring softly, her frail body barely moving under the thin covers.

"Cigarettes to alcohol," he mused darkly. "Cancer's doing all the work for me." There was no pity, no remorse in his thoughts. That part of him had been hollowed out long ago. He only cared about one thing now, the insurance money. "She's doing the job herself," he muttered. "No need to hurry it along."

In the kitchen, he made himself a couple of sandwiches, tossed them into a bag along with some chips and sodas, and headed back upstairs. His mind wandered as he stared at a photograph of Kim. Desire flared up, dark, twisted, and all-consuming. He leaned back in his chair, eyes closed, letting his imagination take over, the forbidden thrill of power and control pulsating through him.

But then, as it always did, the nightmare crept back in. Rejection. The one thing that haunted him more than any dream, more than the devil's grin. It twisted in his gut like a knife.

He left the house quickly, not bothering to check on his mother again. Highway 12 stretched out before him like a path to oblivion. The road was long, 140 miles of nothingness until he reached the city, with three rest stops along the way. It would take patience, but Mick had all the time in the world. After all, the devil waited for him in every shadow, in every dream. And Mick knew, there was no turning back now.

The night was a thick cloak of darkness, draped over Highway 12, stretching north into the vast unknown. Mick's heart thudded in his chest as he cruised along the nearly deserted road. The rest area he'd been waiting for was still miles away, and the anticipation gnawed at him like a wild animal. He imagined it, an isolated stop bathed in dim lights, bordered by nothing but endless fields and the sinister quiet of the night. His fingers drummed on the steering wheel, black pants clinging to his legs like a second skin, as his mind wandered through twisted fantasies of what lay ahead.

As he neared the rest stop 70 miles out, the fading sun gave way to the pitch-black horizon, the air around him growing colder, heavier. The sign for the rest area loomed in the distance, barely illuminated by a faint light flickering overhead. Mick smirked. **Perfect**. He pulled into the truck parking lot, away from the car area, blending into the shadows like a predator preparing to strike. His binoculars were already in hand, surveying the sparse flow of travelers, lone figures, easy prey.

As the minutes dragged on and darkness engulfed the land, fewer and fewer cars rolled in. His stomach churned with the excitement of what was to come, though he forced himself to be patient. **The right one will come. They always do.**

The light near the female bathroom was a nuisance, casting a dim glow that felt like a spotlight aimed directly at him. He couldn't have that. With swift, calculated steps, he approached it. The bulb sat high, but not too high, just eight feet off the ground. He crouched for a moment, gathering his strength, then launched himself up, fist clenched around a small iron ball. The bulb shattered with a soft pop, and the area plunged into near-complete darkness. The thrill of it electrified him; he was invisible now.

Back to the car, waiting, watching. Cars came and went, none meeting the image he had in his mind. **She'll be here soon, he told himself. A white woman, thin, young, someone who looks lost. Someone who won't be missed until it's far too late.** He'd read once how killers like him zero in on specific types, and he had done the same. His hunt was personal, methodical.

It was just past midnight when a sleek, red BMW pulled into the rest stop. Mick's pulse quickened, eyes narrowing on the sleek lines of the car. A man and woman stepped out, her blonde hair gleaming even in the dim light, tight jeans hugging her figure, her white shirt a beacon in the gloom. She yelled something at the man, who disappeared into the male bathroom. She was perfect. Mick's lips curled into a predatory smile.

From his hiding place behind the broken light, he could see her approaching the female bathroom. She was alone. The hunter in him stirred, the adrenaline rushing through his veins. He needed her to come out before the man did, and every second of waiting felt like a lifetime. **Come on, come on,** he thought, fists clenched.

And then the door opened. She stepped out, looking back toward the men's bathroom, the coast clear. She moved quickly toward the BMW, and Mick saw his chance.

He was on her in an instant, moving silently through the dark like a shadow. She didn't hear him, didn't see him, until it was too late. The iron ball smashed into her head with a sickening thud, and she crumpled, the scream caught in her throat before it could escape. His other arm snaked around her slender frame, lifting her like a rag doll. She was lighter than he expected, no more than 120 pounds, maybe less. He dragged her limp body back to his car, the darkness hiding his every move.

He shoved her into the backseat, quickly snapping handcuffs around her wrists. There was no time to admire his prize, not yet. He slid into the driver's seat, heart still pounding, hands shaking with the rush of it all. As he pulled away, he glanced toward the men's bathroom, still no sign of the man. **Must be taking his sweet time.** Mick chuckled under his breath, a low, guttural sound.

The car hummed as it sped down Highway 12, back toward the dark stretch of road from which he came. He kept the speed steady, not wanting to attract attention, but his mind raced. His eyes flicked back to the rearview mirror, where the woman lay unconscious, her chest rising and falling in shallow breaths. The sight of her, bound and helpless, sent a surge of satisfaction through him.

But it wasn't enough. The hunger inside him, the one that had driven him to this moment, gnawed relentlessly at him. **This is just the beginning**, he thought, his grip tightening on the steering wheel. He had her now, but what came next? What twisted fate awaited her? His imagination ran wild with possibilities, each darker and more grotesque than the last.

Mick's pulse quickened as he thought about the remote place he'd scouted, a hidden cabin, miles from anywhere. No one would hear her scream. No one would come looking for her in time.

8

Patterns

Mick sat hunched over in his worn recliner, eyes locked onto the flickering screen. The local news played on, the same mundane headlines rolling by, but his mind was elsewhere. It was almost a year since Melissa's death, and the echoes of her disappearance had begun to fade from public consciousness. Commercials and half-hearted news segments were dwindling, but he could still feel their presence like a ghost in the back of his mind. Would they ever stop? He didn't know if he wanted them to.

The unsolved cases of three missing women loomed over the region like a dark cloud. Three women, vanishing within a hundred-mile radius over the span of a year, and yet, the authorities hadn't pieced it together, not entirely. Mick knew the police weren't stupid; they were methodical, like sharks circling their prey. But he was smarter. He had kept things tight, kept his secrets buried deep. For now, he was in no immediate danger. But that could change in a heartbeat.

Mick had become his own investigator, tracing their steps, watching the aftermath with fascination. He knew their ages, their faces, their names. Except for the blonde, her name had slipped through his fingers. She had no ID, no purse, no trace of herself except her body, now long gone. The day he took her, two weeks ago, was still fresh in his mind. He could recall every detail, down to the way the hunting knife felt in his hand as he sliced her clothes off in the dark, abandoned parking lot.

He had hit her hard, harder than he realized. She groaned, coughed, a sound that sent a shock through him. Her eyes never opened, though, her consciousness dancing on the edge of oblivion as he took her. The memory of that moment still burned hot, a molten imprint searing his thoughts. His orgasm had been seismic, like an eruption shaking the very core of his being. But even that had faded, just like the others. The high, the gratification, it all slipped away too quickly. And now, the itch was back.

The news droned on in the background, offering nothing about the missing women, no new leads. Mick smirked to himself. **"Three women,"** he whispered, as if speaking it aloud gave him more power. **"Three lives snuffed out by my hand."** He sat there, reveling in the twisted pride that swelled within him. **"I'm a serial killer."** The words echoed in his mind, as if claiming that identity gave him an authority he'd never felt before.

Most murders were sloppy, born of passion, anger, or some petty dispute between people who knew each other. Not Mick. His kills were clean, detached, almost clinical. There was no connection between him and his victims. They were strangers, nameless faces that simply ceased to exist after he was through with them. And that, he knew, made him nearly impossible to catch.

Society loved serial killers, didn't they? They were fascinated by the horror of it all, the psychologists and cops who tried to untangle the minds of these monsters. But none of them really understood, none of them could possibly know the raw, primal **power** that surged through Mick every time he took a life.

At night, he prowled. A beast in the darkness, his eyes gleaming with the hunger of a predator. He moved silently through the shadows, his mind consumed with fantasies of domination, of control. The anticipation was almost as thrilling as the act itself, the hunt, the **power**. It made him feel alive in a way nothing else ever had. His hands tingled with the memory of their softness, his pulse quickened as the predator inside him growled for more.

Would he ever be caught? The thought slipped into his mind, unbidden. **"Probably,"** he muttered under his breath. But it didn't matter, not really. Stopping was never an option. The need was too strong, the desire too overwhelming. His very soul vibrated with the anticipation of his next kill.

There was something broken inside Mick, something that twisted him into what he had become. He knew that. The psychologists would call it antisocial behavior. **"Psychopathy,"** maybe, if they ever got their hands on him. But none of that mattered to him. He didn't care about their labels, their diagnoses. All he knew was that he lacked something other people seemed to have: empathy, remorse, even fear. Those emotions didn't exist for him.

He remembered Melissa, the first. The one who started it all. He had wanted her for so long, had asked her out so many times, only to be rejected, over and over. But that night, she came to him, willingly, for **entertainment**, nothing more. The cops never suspected him, never even questioned him about her disappearance. His obsession with her remained his secret. She was the first, and from her, he had learned. Rejection would no longer be his burden; it would be theirs.

His mother had been in bed more often lately, resting, sleeping. He checked on her out of habit, but it wasn't love that motivated him. It was a duty. He had to keep up appearances, had to play the part of the caring son. But in truth, she was nothing more than a burden, a barrier between him and his freedom. He wondered how much longer she had. Her life insurance would solve so many of his problems. When she was gone, everything would be his.

A smile crept across his face as he thought about it. He could sell the house, take the money, and disappear. Move across the country, start fresh, maybe even find new hunting grounds. He had always loved maps, and he spent hours poring over them, imagining where he might go next. Arizona? Texas? Florida? Each place held its own possibilities, its own unique challenges. He could reinvent himself, vanish into a new life, and the cycle could begin again.

Later that night, Mick found himself restless. The sun was setting, casting long, eerie shadows across his quiet neighborhood. He slipped out of the house, a three-inch metal ball juggled between his hands as he walked, his mind alive with possibilities. There was a full moon overhead, illuminating the streets in an unnatural glow. It was the perfect night for a hunt.

There were women nearby who fit his type. He knew that. He had seen them, watched them from afar, but something held him back. **Be cautious**, he reminded himself. Killing too close to home would be reckless. He had to be smart; he had to think like the predator he was. Leave clues, but not too many. Be meticulous, be patient.

When he returned home, his mother was still asleep. He lingered by her door for a moment, listening to her soft, uneven breathing. He felt nothing as he turned and headed upstairs, his mind already drifting back to the maps, to the women, to the hunt.

The night wore on, and as Mick sat in his small, dimly lit room, the urge within him began to fade. But it never vanished completely. It was always there, lurking just beneath the surface, waiting to rise again. He would kill again. He knew that as surely as he knew the sun would rise the next morning.

The thrill, the arousal, the **power**, it was all-consuming. And as he finally drifted off to sleep, he knew the devil was watching, smiling, waiting for him to make his next move.

Morning came, and with it, a faint sound. Mick awoke slowly, his senses still dulled by sleep. But then he heard it again, his mother's voice, weak and fragile.

"Mick... call an ambulance."

He sprinted towards his phone, his heart pounding not with fear, but with anticipation.

9

Town in Fear

Andrew Taylor's head throbbed as he pulled into the parking lot of the precinct. The glare of the morning sun reflected off the windshield, stabbing into his still-hazy vision. It had been two days since the wedding anniversary party of a close friend, and he was still feeling the aftereffects of too much liquor and too little sleep. He muttered to himself, gripping the steering wheel tightly as he parked, "Fifteen years on the force, and I still haven't learned when to stop drinking."

The precinct loomed large and uninviting, a recent addition to the city's growing infrastructure. The sterile concrete walls seemed to echo the weight of the crimes Andrew had spent years trying to solve. Walking inside, he glanced at the secretary's desk as he passed by.

"Good morning, Lizz," Andrew said, forcing a smile. "Can you get me a coffee? No sugar, all black."

"Morning, Andy," Lizz replied, cheerful as ever. "Sure thing, I'll bring it right to your office."

Andrew barely acknowledged her as he strode past, heading towards his newly renovated office. He appreciated the change from the old bullpen setup, where officers were stacked on top of each other like cattle. Now, he had his own space, his own corner to gather his thoughts amidst the madness. But as much as the new digs were an improvement, the horrors of the job followed him no matter where he sat.

He placed his papers and notebooks neatly on his desk, taking a moment to steady himself. His mind wandered back to the missing person cases that had been piling up on his desk. Young women, all around the same age, all disappearing without a trace. No bodies. No witnesses. Nothing.

The door creaked open, and Lizz entered with his coffee, placing it in front of him.

"Officer Campbell has a Zoom meeting with you at 9 a.m.," she reminded him. "Something about those cases you've been working on."

"I know," Andrew replied, his voice gravelly from exhaustion. "Thanks for the coffee, Lizz."

She left without another word, the door clicking shut behind her. Andrew sighed and closed his eyes for a brief moment, allowing the darkness to swallow him. How had things become so complicated? He had children of his own, and every day, the dread gnawed at him. What kind of world was he leaving for them? A world where monsters lurked in the shadows, unseen but all too real?

He snapped back to reality as his computer chimed, 8:58 a.m. It was time. He opened his email, found the Zoom link, and clicked to join the meeting. The familiar screen appeared, and soon, the tired face of Officer Paul Campbell filled his monitor.

"Good morning, Andrew," Paul said, his voice flat but professional.

"Morning, Paul. How are you doing?"

"Doing fine, thanks." Paul glanced down at a sheet of paper in front of him. "Listen, I've been looking at your record, 94% of your collars have ended up behind bars. That's impressive. You're one of the most ethical and principled detectives we have on the force."

Andrew shifted in his chair. Compliments never sat well with him. "Just doing my job," he muttered.

"Well, we need someone like you on this. Let's cut to the chase, within a 120-mile radius of the city, five people have gone missing over the last year. Two of them were children, one of whom was found. The remaining three are women, all white, ages 18 to 27. No bodies, no leads."

Andrew felt a pit form in his stomach as Paul continued.

"The first woman, a high school student, vanished without a trace. The second was last seen at a bar; her car was still in the parking lot, but she wasn't. The third disappeared at a rest stop on Highway 12. Her boyfriend went to the restroom, and when he came back, she was gone."

Andrew's mind raced as Paul laid out the grim facts. He had heard these stories before, cold cases with no bodies to mourn, no clues to follow. The worst kind of cases. His instincts screamed at him that this was the work of a serial killer.

"You think this is one person?" Andrew asked, his voice low.

"We have to assume so," Paul replied. "There's no solid evidence yet, but the pattern is too strong to ignore. Whoever it is, they're organized. They have a plan."

Andrew leaned back in his chair, the weight of the unsolved cases pressing down on him. He had seen this before: women vanishing, their families left in a state of perpetual limbo, wondering if their daughters, sisters, or wives were alive or dead. More often than not, they were already gone.

Paul's voice broke through Andrew's thoughts. "Look, we'll give you all the resources you need. Helicopters, FBI involvement, whatever it takes. But we both know how this usually ends. By percentage, these women are probably already dead."

Andrew's eyes darkened. "I'll do everything I can, Paul. That's a promise."

The meeting ended, and Andrew sat alone in his office, staring at the files on his desk. Three missing women, no leads, and a killer still out there. Somewhere. Watching. Waiting.

Across town, Priest Gary Brown had just returned to his small, modest church. He loved the building, with its large windows that let in sunlight, casting warmth across the pews. The light always felt like a blessing, a sign that no matter the darkness, hope could still shine through.

He had just finished a paper on human behavior, a study on narcissism and the lack of accountability in modern society. He was proud of the work, examining the thin line between cruelty born of evil and cruelty born of madness. There was a difference, he believed, between inhuman acts committed by those who had lost their minds and those who chose to walk the path of malevolence.

As Gary made his way down the hall, he saw Priest David Stewart approaching. "Hi, David," Gary greeted him warmly.

"Gary," David replied with a nod. "How was class?"

"Enlightening. I always enjoy learning more about the human mind," Gary said with a smile.

"Maybe I should take some classes," David mused. "I'd love to expand my understanding."

"You should," Gary encouraged him. "You'd enjoy it."

As David continued down the hall, Gary walked to the end of the corridor, where the large windows offered a view of the street below. He loved these moments of stillness, the sun filtering in through the glass. It made him feel connected to something greater, something peaceful.

But as he gazed out, something caught his eye, a figure standing on the sidewalk, looking up at him. It was a man, short and stout, dressed in a three-piece suit and a bowler hat. The man's face was obscured by the shadow of the hat, but Gary could feel his gaze, piercing and unsettling.

The man lifted his hat in a strange gesture, a formal bow that sent a chill down Gary's spine. Then, without a word, the man replaced his hat and walked away, disappearing into the city's labyrinth of streets.

Gary blinked, unsure of what he had just witnessed. "Odd," he muttered to himself, stepping back from the window.

But the image of the man stayed with him, the unnatural way he had moved, the silent bow that felt like a mockery of politeness. Something was wrong. Deeply wrong.

10

The Cost of Waiting

The fluorescent lights above flickered faintly, casting an unnatural pallor over the hospital's sterile walls. The air was thick with the smell of antiseptic, masking the reality of sickness and slow decay. Mick sat across from Dr. Richards in a small, dimly lit room that barely contained the weight of the conversation. The doctor's voice was measured, almost too calm for the storm raging inside Mick's head.

"Lung cancer surgery is an option for patients depending on the type, location, and stage," Dr. Richards began, his words slow and deliberate. "But that's the problem we're facing. It's advanced... Dr. Walker and I believe it may be spreading rapidly."

Mick's stomach tightened. The words hung in the air like smoke, curling around him, suffocating. Spreading rapidly. The phrase echoed in his mind, growing darker with each repetition. There was no escape from this. Not for his mother. And certainly not for him.

The doctor continued, his voice like a distant hum as if speaking from the far end of a tunnel. "Attempts to cure or hold back lung cancer with surgery involve removing the tumor along with some surrounding tissue, including lymph nodes in the region of the tumor itself. This is best done in the early stages of the disease." He paused, and for a moment, the silence pressed in on them both.

"But the other doctors and I think it may be too late for that now."

Mick stared blankly, his mind trying to latch onto something, anything, that made this feel less final. But it didn't. The situation was slipping through his fingers like sand, and all he could do was sit there, feeling the weight of it pull him under.

The doctor's voice sharpened as he went on, "She used to smoke heavily, didn't she?"

"Yeah," Mick muttered, barely audible.

"That's what I thought. She gave up smoking, but from what I understand, she's been drinking quite a bit too." The doctor's tone darkened. "That's adding another problem, her liver, kidneys... they're all struggling."

A wave of dread washed over Mick. His mother, frail and dying, was lying just a few rooms away, her body betraying her after years of self-destruction. The booze had eroded her like acid, leaving behind a hollow shell. And now this cancer, growing inside her like some malevolent force, was claiming what little was left.

"She's medicated right now," Dr. Richards said softly. "Asleep. But even when she's awake, it's stiff trying to get answers from her. She's... resistant. Doesn't want to talk about what comes next. She's barely able to give us a clear direction."

The words "resistant" struck Mick. His mother had always been like that, stubborn, fighting tooth and nail against anything that threatened her control. Even now, as death circled closer, she wouldn't surrender.

"You're her only family, Mick. It's tough, I know. You don't have to make a decision right now, but... we could let things go as they are." The doctor's voice lowered, "No surgery. Use medicinal treatment until..."

"Until there's nothing left," Mick finished the sentence for him, his voice hollow. He understood the code. It meant letting her die slowly, but comfortably. Or as comfortably as one could, tethered to tubes and machines, watching the clock run out.

"I'm sorry, Mick," the doctor said, placing a hand on his shoulder in a gesture meant to offer comfort. But it felt like the weight of finality.

Mick nodded, keeping his face neutral. He couldn't break now. He couldn't let the cracks show. Not here. Not yet. The doctor walked away, leaving him alone with his thoughts. Thoughts that were far from those of a grieving son.

His mother's life insurance policy flashed in his mind. The payout would be significant. After all, what good was a life of chain-smoking, cheap wine, and bitter arguments if it didn't leave something behind? Mick had already called the insurance company once, just to confirm everything was in place. The woman on the other end had been so polite, so understanding. How little she knew.

Mick exhaled slowly, as if trying to exorcise the sick satisfaction creeping through his veins. "I think my acting is pretty damn good," he thought with a bitter smile. "The loving, sorrowful son... ready to weep over his poor mother's impending death."

But there would be no tears. Not from him. Not unless they were crocodile tears to play the part. And as long as the insurance check arrived promptly, he could endure the charade.

He stepped out of the room and into the waiting area. A small group of his mother's friends had gathered there, their faces lined with concern and sadness. The air felt different around them, heavy with genuine sorrow, a stark contrast to the dark calculus ticking away in Mick's brain.

Amy, a longtime friend of his mother, approached him with a soft, sympathetic smile. "We thought we'd come by and see your mom, but the nurses said she's asleep right now. I'm so sorry, Mick," she whispered as she wrapped her arms around him.

Her hug was warm and comforting. But Mick didn't hug her back. His arms hung limp by his sides. He felt nothing except a distant awareness of her breasts pressing against his chest. His mind went to dark places, places he shouldn't let it wander to. She was in her fifties, but still attractive in a way that stirred something in him, a sick desire he couldn't shake.

Closing his eyes, he tried to focus. "Control yourself, Mick. You're in a hospital. Act like the grieving son, damn it," he thought, forcing himself to put on a mask of sorrow.

He finally returned the hug, giving Amy a brief squeeze before stepping back. "Thank you, Amy," he murmured, his voice deliberately low, sad. The others nodded sympathetically, their expressions full of concern.

"We all love your mom, Mick. If there's anything we can do, just let us know," Amy said, her eyes full of kindness.

Mick swallowed, trying to keep up the act. "The doctors haven't told me much yet," he lied. He didn't want to talk about it. "But... my gut tells me it's not going well." The others exchanged looks, their faces filled with unspoken dread.

"Well, we're going to grab some lunch. Thought we'd stop by and check in first," Amy said softly, glancing at the door to Mick's mother's room.

"Thank you," Mick said again, his voice barely above a whisper. "You all take care."

They said their goodbyes and headed for the exit, leaving Mick alone with his thoughts once more. He slumped into a chair, rubbing his face with his hands. He had missed most of his college classes over the past few days. Maybe they'd let him retake the exams. Not that it mattered. All that really mattered was the insurance payout.

The ticking of the clock filled the silence as Mick wandered back into his mother's room. She looked like a ghost. Her pale face was almost unrecognizable, her body frail and sunken beneath the weight of disease and decay. The respirator's soft hiss was the only sign that life still clung to her, however weakly.

A nurse stood by her bedside, checking the machines. She glanced up when Mick entered.

"Are you her son?" she asked, her voice quiet, as if speaking too loudly might disturb the fragile balance between life and death.

"Yes," Mick replied, staring at the lifeless form in the bed.

"She didn't sleep very well last night, so she might be out for a while," the nurse said quietly.

"That's fine," Mick replied, glancing down the hallway. "I could use some fresh air anyway." As the nurse moved on to tend to other patients, Mick stepped outside and headed toward his car.

He drove aimlessly for a while before pulling into the Plymouth Theatre parking lot. The comedy playing had been in the theater for weeks, so the place was nearly empty. He sat in the back row, with only a few scattered people in front of him. Even when the jokes fell flat, Mick laughed louder than anyone else in the theater. It was the kind of laughter that didn't come from humor but from something else, an attempt to escape, to release tension he didn't want to acknowledge.

Andrew stared at the paperwork in front of him, his mind turning over the endless studies he had read on human behavior, psychological disorders, trauma, emotional shock, all of it. He'd been in classrooms before, studying the science of the mind, antisocial personalities, stressors, and the long-lasting effects of childhood trauma. Yet none of it seemed to fully explain what drove someone to become a serial killer.

The facts he had in front of him were few but pointed. Serial killers, typically male, often had strange relationships with their mothers, if you could call them relationships at all. And paraphilias, those disturbing, atypical turn-ons? Men were statistically more prone to them than women. Andrew believed there had to be more to it, something rooted in DNA, the very essence of a person. If behavior was partly genetic, shouldn't there be a way to catch these killers before they started down the path of violence?

He thumbed through the sparse collection of documents. Most of it was repetitive, offering no real leads, just theories that did little to help capture a predator. "Maybe serial killers are just getting better at hiding their crimes," Andrew muttered under his breath.

Three women missing. That was all he had to go on. He stared down at the first file: Melissa. The logic told him that the first kidnapping was likely the least experienced; the killer might have known her. He combed through the details again, slowly, fact by fact. Ashland, a town of 56,292 people. Melissa had been last seen at Roosevelt School. White male, between 18 and 30, his pool of suspects had already been narrowed down to about one in ten thousand.

Melissa was the first victim. She had come from a wealthy family, had just started college, her future bright. Her parents had seen her on the morning she disappeared, then, in an instant, she was gone. Her mother was a wreck; the officers who questioned her noted how she had been drinking before they even arrived. Desperation poured from every word she spoke, begging for someone to find her daughter.

Andrew considered re-interviewing the people in Ashland, but he doubted he'd get anything new. Every question that could be asked had already been exhausted.

The second woman had been taken from a bar, Pint and Peanuts. Friends and the bartender saw her, but no one noticed when she left. Her car remained in the parking lot, meaning she had been abducted just outside, possibly from the exit. She was 27, brunette, and attractive.

The third victim, another blonde, 25 years old, had disappeared from a rest area off Highway 12.

Andrew closed his eyes and tried to map it out in his head. The first woman disappeared around 3:30 p.m., the second after 10 p.m., and the third vanished after 1 a.m. Three different times, three different settings, yet they were all too carefully planned. This killer didn't act on impulse. He had a strategy. Every abduction was precise, well-timed, and methodical. Andrew's gut screamed at him that these women were dead.

"This guy won't do anything without a plan," Andrew muttered. "He's careful, but luck runs out. Sooner or later, someone will see something."

He knew the next step would be to get the women's pictures on TV, offer a reward for any leads. His gut told him the outcome, but protocol had to be followed. He just hoped they could stop the killer before another woman disappeared.

Priest Gary Brown sipped his brandy slowly, staring into the amber liquid. Across from him, Priest David Stewart swirled his own glass, the two men sitting in a comfortable silence, having known each other since they were teenagers.

"Thanks for the drink, David," Gary said, setting his glass down. "But I'm not feeling too well."

David raised an eyebrow. "If you're not feeling well, brandy might not be the best choice."

"No, it's not that," Gary sighed. "Physically, I'm fine. It's just... I've got this feeling, you know? A gut feeling."

David leaned forward. "What kind of feeling?"

"I don't know, maybe it's nothing. I've had it before, though. It's like this... a sense that something's coming. Something big."

David nodded knowingly. "I get it. You've talked about this sixth sense before, haven't you? Like a warning?"

Gary chuckled. "Yeah, I suppose I have. It's like a shift is coming, something or someone that's going to change my life."

David smiled. "I get it. Sometimes, the world just seems to weigh on you. There's so much darkness mixed with love. Just think about it, thousands of children starving, suffering. It's enough to make anyone feel something deep inside."

11

Unfinished Business

The room was thick with an eerie silence as Mick sat beside his mother, her face pallid and drawn under the dull hospital lighting. She gripped his hand, cold and frail, her cough rattling like a haunted whisper as she struggled to speak.

"Mick...hello Mick," she murmured, her voice a paper-thin rasp. Her hand trembled, fingers curling weakly around his. "Take my hand."

Mick glanced at her, his mind spinning with resentment tangled with pity. He held her hand, feeling the frailty of her bones, as she wheezed out a painful breath.

"How is my little baby doing?" she asked, smiling faintly, though even that seemed to pain her.

"I'm fine, Mom," he replied, forcing warmth into his tone. But inside, his thoughts were cold. *Now you're kind*, he thought bitterly. *Now, when you're dying, you soften.*

"You look a lot better than you did a few days ago," he lied, watching her struggle to keep her eyes open, her face growing more ghostly with each second.

"Oh... I feel awesome," she whispered with a fragile cough that left her clutching her chest. Mick watched her, a sense of finality settling over him, as if her spirit was fading in front of his eyes. "You have a girlfriend yet?" she asked, forcing out the words with effort. "I always wanted... a grandchild."

Mick's mind flicked back to the years of coldness, her sharp words, the hollowness of his childhood. He met her gaze, deadpan. "Sorry, Mom, that probably won't happen."

He watched her eyes drift away, her mouth hanging open slightly as she wheezed, each breath a whispered plea for release.

Later, Mick returned home, feeling a weight lift as he distanced himself from her waning presence. Alone in the dark, he grilled a couple of pork chops, barely tasting them as he chewed, his mind drifting to his own obsessions. Outside, night descended, wrapping around the house like a shroud. The darkness was his friend, his refuge from the expectations, the pity, the pleas for absolution.

Throwing on black pants, a black shirt, and gloves, he took a sleek metal ball in his hand, tossing it back and forth, relishing the heavy, solid feel of it. Darkness cloaked him, shrouding his steps as he prowled through the empty streets, shifting his path each night. Each step brought him deeper into the inky abyss, where his face blurred into the shadows and his footsteps vanished into silence.

As he moved through the quiet neighborhood, he saw Mrs. Renfeld unloading groceries. She heaved bags from her car, her figure framed by the harsh beam of her porch light. Mick melted into the shade of a nearby tree, watching her scurry back and forth like a trapped animal. His lips twisted into a slight smile as he observed her, feeling the thrill of invisibility, of being nothing but a dark specter watching from the shadows.

He slipped away unnoticed, walking back to his house with a grin that grew as the shadows deepened. Alone, his thoughts drifted to the objects cluttering his mother's home, the trinkets she valued so much. "I'll sell it all," he thought, walking through the quiet halls. "A garage sale for the worthless junk, and the jewelry, I'll pawn that. Just wait for the insurance check. Let her things disappear like she will."

That night, he drifted into a fitful sleep. In his dreams, he found himself at the base of a mountain, the ground glowing with molten magma that spilled down the slopes like liquid fire. Along the base, hundreds of people were chained, their faces twisted in torment, their voices rising in silent screams. Waves of blood-red water crashed against a rocky shore nearby, drowning their cries under the thunderous roar.

And there, towering above them, was the Devil himself, his skin a sickly crimson, wings stretching like jagged shadows against the sky. He stalked among the tormented souls, his eyes gleaming with a malevolent glee as he pointed at each of them.

"Your vanity, your greed, your selfishness…" His voice thundered like an inferno as he roared accusations at them. "You chose this! You fed this darkness!"

The Devil's eyes snapped to Mick, his face contorting into a grotesque grin. With a flap of his massive wings, he shot forward, his face inches from Mick's own. His expression twisted into something both familiar and horrifying, and in his hand, he held a hypodermic needle, a foot long, its point glinting in the molten glow.

Mick tried to scream, but no sound escaped his lips. The Devil leaned closer, winking as he raised the needle, its point aimed straight at Mick's heart.

And then Mick jolted awake, drenched in a cold sweat. His room was silent, the shadows thick around him, but he could still feel the Devil's eyes, watching from the darkness, waiting.

12

The Dark Hunger

Mick exited the library at Dunwoods, adjusting his bag as he stepped into the warm afternoon light. The wind rustled through the trees, casting dancing shadows on the pavement as he paused, momentarily staring off into the distance. His mom had been moved to a treatment center run by the American Cancer Society, located just south of the city. He didn't mind the arrangement; it gave him the house to himself, a place that would soon be solely his.

Three months had passed since she had moved in. The treatment center offered a type of care she cherished, nurses managing her needs rather than relying on herself or, worse, Mick. He visited often, making the trip out three or four times a week. Their conversations, however, were anything but profound. Words hovered on the surface, never dipping into the emotions buried beneath. Sara, his mom, preferred it that way, even though Mick often wondered what they could be saying if they only tried.

As he began walking away from the library, he spotted Kim. She was leaving the building too, her long red hair catching the sunlight.

"Hi, Kim," he called out, a small smile forcing its way onto his face.

"Mick!" she replied, surprised. "Haven't seen you around here for a while."

"I've been around," he responded, shrugging slightly. "Classes and... other things, you know."

Kim's face softened as she nodded. "I know, Mick. Your mom has lung cancer." They held each other's gaze for a moment, words hanging unspoken between them. Mick felt a dull pang, a strange mix of guilt and indifference. His mom's illness wasn't something he wanted or willed, yet... he couldn't find the depth of sadness that others might expect.

Kim's voice broke the silence. "I'm sorry, Mick. Your family has done so much for this school. We're all here for you." Her gaze lingered, and her words carried a depth of sincerity.

"Thank you, Kim," he replied. "I'm grateful for being here, for learning... and for people like you."

She smiled, her eyes warm. "Be sure to tell her I said hi when you see her."

He nodded. "Will do. You have a good day, Kim."

Watching her walk away, he couldn't help but fixate on her. There was something captivating about her, the fluidity of her movements, the way her long legs strode with effortless grace. He knew he felt something primal, a pull toward her that he couldn't ignore. "Her kindness means nothing to me," he thought, "but her beauty, her presence, that does." His mind wandered, enthralled by her every curve and graceful line, unable to look away until she finally rounded the corner and disappeared from view.

Mick let out a deep breath and made his way to his car. A gnawing hunger crept up on him, urging him back to the house. Once home, he found some hamburger patties in the freezer and fired up the grill. He threw on a small TV in the kitchen for background noise, the same routine news humming in the background as he worked. His attention sharpened when a local news segment interrupted the dull chatter.

"The city of Ashland and surrounding areas continue the search for three missing young women," the anchor announced, a sense of urgency in her voice. Images of three girls flashed on the screen: Melissa, Evelyn, and Molly. The reward of $50,000 was tempting any residents with clues to step forward. Mick's eyes lingered on Molly's picture, the name whispered aloud as if he could feel her memory haunting the room.

"They've got nothing," he muttered, a twisted smile tugging at his lips as the commercial faded into other ads. He turned his focus back to his meal, practically yelling to himself, "They got nothing!"

After a quiet dinner of burgers, chips, and beans, he cleaned up and decided he should go visit his mom. He wondered idly about the cost of her treatment, something that had increasingly weighed on his mind. Once he got to the center, it looked the same as always: nurses bustling, rooms quiet, the sterile smell clinging to the air.

As he approached his mom's room, he saw two nurses inside, struggling to calm her down. She was thrashing, her arms swinging wildly, incoherent words spilling from her lips between thick coughs. Her face was a mask of fear and confusion.

"Mick… hold my hand," she rasped through her coughs as her eyes caught sight of him. One of the nurses stepped aside, letting Mick take her trembling hand.

"Mom, are you okay?" he asked, leaning close. Her grip tightened, strength ebbing from her as she continued to cough.

"Just having you here, Mick," she managed through her labored breaths. "It helps… makes me feel… relaxed."

"Rest, Mom," he murmured, feeling a strange urge to tell her something genuine. "I love you."

"Love you too," she whispered, her voice faint as one of the nurses injected her IV with two syringes, one to ease her pain, the other to let sleep finally take over. As she drifted off, her breathing mask was placed gently over her face.

After a quick conversation with one of the nurses about her deteriorating health, Mick left. He spent the drive home in silence, thoughts drifting to his own life. Once back at the house, he wandered from room to room, assessing which items he'd keep and which he'd discard. His dad's old tools, cabinets, and tables were untouchable; they held memories he valued, unlike his mother's things, which would mostly be sold off or given away.

Later, upstairs in his room, Mick opened his notebook, glancing at the small list he had of his previous victims: blonde, brunette, blonde. No trophies kept, but memories lingered. Molly's face flashed through his mind again, her innocence, her sweetness, and he felt a surge of twisted pride, the dark satisfaction gnawing at him. It was the only time he'd taken a step further, and the experience had been electric, consuming him with a thrill that felt almost divine. But that fulfillment was fleeting, a hunger that only grew stronger, clawing at him with increasing desperation. Four months since his last taste of that forbidden high. He knew the need would return soon, stronger than before, and with it, a fierce, undeniable urge.

The phone's shrill ring jolted him awake early the next morning. Groggy, he reached for it. "Hello?"

"Mick, this is Robyn from the treatment center," came the voice, soft but laced with tension.

"Yes, Robyn, I remember you," he said, his voice steady.

There was a pause, a painful hesitation before she spoke again. "Mick... I'm so sorry. It's your mother, she's gone."

He felt the words settle heavily over him, yet his response was void of surprise. "I know," he whispered, the strange calm washing over him as he realized just how little he felt.

13

A Call for Witnesses

Andrew Taylor sank deeply into his worn leather chair, eyes fixed on the hockey game flashing across the TV screen. He sipped his coffee and checked the clock, mentally calculating the minutes until the commercial would air. Hockey had always been his escape, but tonight he felt a dark, creeping anxiety; his thoughts were wrapped around the disturbing case that had consumed his last few months. Three women abducted, all vanished without a trace from the area, and despite every lead and theory, nothing had brought them closer to the truth.

He'd recently reached out to KTHI, the local news station, pressing for a public appeal. They'd compiled recent, sharp photos of each woman, eyes, faces, expressions vivid on the screen, and details of the last places they were seen. The commercial was intended to make these women unforgettable to anyone who watched, urging the community to come forward with any information, however small. The reward for information leading to an arrest was a hefty $50,000, a staggering sum that Andrew knew would stir up more than just serious tips. He braced himself for the deluge of irrelevant calls he knew would follow.

"Here we go," he thought, fingers drumming nervously on the armrest. In his years of experience, he'd learned that many tip-offs, well-meaning as they may be, often led nowhere. But this time, it was different. The stakes were higher. Every day without a credible lead could mean the difference between life and death for these women, if they were even still alive.

Andrew closed his eyes, feeling the weight of his own doubts pressing down. *"My gut tells me these women are gone,"* he murmured under his breath. He knew that, statistically, after this much time had passed, the odds were grim. *"If this guy's even halfway smart, we may never see them again, at least not alive."* The chilling thought held him captive, and he felt a surge of helpless frustration. Serial killers were often egotistical, prone to eventual mistakes, but how many more would suffer before that happened?

Meanwhile, in a quiet basement kitchen of a nearby church, Priests David Brown and Gary Stewart sipped their coffee, chatting between bites of their sandwiches. David had always enjoyed these late evening talks with Gary, a recent psychology student fascinated by human behavior.

"So, how many papers have you written so far?" David asked, leaning back and grinning.

"Only two," Gary replied, laughing softly. "Writing's tougher than I thought, so much groundwork before you can even start putting thoughts to paper. It's not easy making sense of what drives people to certain behaviors, let alone trying to explain it to others."

David nodded thoughtfully, taking a sip of his coffee. "You know, psychology's always interested me. I might even go back to school myself, maybe study mental processes, personality, get a little insight into what makes people tick."

Their conversation was interrupted by a sudden hush that spread across the room. Glancing toward the small TV in the corner, David noticed several others had turned to watch a new commercial. He squinted at the images, three young women's faces flashed on screen, each accompanied by brief details: their names, the dates, and locations of their disappearances. David's heart tightened as he watched, the reality of the recent kidnappings settling heavily into the quiet of the room.

Priest Gary shifted uneasily, his mind flickering between academic theories and the stark reality on the screen. David looked at him, curiosity in his eyes. "Gary, is this the kind of thing you study? I mean, what drives someone to do…something like this?"

Gary exhaled, thoughtfully. "Well…yes. Crimes like these often involve people who lack empathy or who have a deep need for control. The question is, is it mental illness, or is it something darker? Personal choice, maybe?" He was hesitant, not wanting to admit how close to home this struck. Part of him felt drawn to understand, to solve the puzzle, even as it repulsed him.

David chuckled, breaking the somber mood. "You could be a detective, you know, help the cops catch the guy." He laughed, but there was a lingering tension in his voice.

Gary laughed back, but uneasily. "I doubt I'll ever meet someone that evil," he said, though as he looked back at the TV screen, a shiver ran down his spine. Somewhere, he felt, something sinister was stirring.

And elsewhere, a figure in the dark watched the world around him with a smug smile.

14

And She Goes

Mick watched as the black hearse pulled up in front of the church, its polished exterior gleaming like dark glass in the midday sun. The ornate building before him, a gleaming beacon of faith and tradition, stood in sharp contrast to his tumultuous mind. As his mother's casket was lifted by cousins he barely recognized, he kept his face carefully expressionless. A mask. He had perfected that, the act of looking puzzled, or somber, or curious, whatever the moment demanded. He could not summon a tear, not even for show. The emotions others seemed to feel so easily eluded him; even now, he couldn't comprehend their authenticity.

The church held a peculiar beauty for him, as it had since he was a boy. Back then, he'd come here every Wednesday for classes, sitting in the cool stillness of the nave, listening to the words of the Father and the cleric. They'd speak of faith, love, and the struggle between good and evil, concepts he had never fully understood or felt. He used to wonder if they wanted him to make up his own mind about these ideas or simply obey, to believe as he was told without questioning. Now, as an adult, he had only begun to grasp the intensity of these concepts, but not in the way they had likely intended.

As he sat on a bench outside, the church's familiar grandeur was almost comforting, though it failed to reach the depths where his thoughts twisted darkly. His mind drifted to that encounter, his first kill. The Devil himself had appeared in that moment, or so the creature claimed. He could still picture the knife as it sliced, feeling the raw satisfaction of severing flesh, only to watch in shock as the wounds healed as if nothing had happened. "The Devil," Mick thought. "He must be real, or else that cut wouldn't have sealed up so quick."

The parking lot was filling up, mostly with his mother's friends and distant family on his father's side. People lingered around, exchanging soft words and sharing memories, dressed in black, their faces lined with grief and sympathy. Mick observed them from his bench, feeling a detachment that seemed as absolute as it was unbreakable. He knew that, by society's standards, his actions were vile, evil even. But as he mused on this, he felt a defiant spark. "Who decides what's good and what's evil anyway?" he thought. "From where I'm standing, it's just a matter of time and convenience, and I'll do whatever it takes to keep my truth hidden. The police will claw at the edges, sniffing around, but they'll find nothing."

His gaze shifted toward the entrance as Amy emerged from the church. Sara's best friend looked stunning even in dark, somber clothes. Despite the modest attire, her form was apparent to him; he saw beauty in its rawest sense, a primal appreciation that quickly transformed into a desire to possess, to end her allure. Amy made her way over, offering him a sympathetic smile. "Hi Mick," she said softly, sitting beside him. "I'm so sorry. She died too soon."

"Yes, I know," he replied, his voice flat yet polite. Amy's words blended into the background noise as she tried to offer him comfort. She mentioned how his mother had been proud of him, how she'd talk about him now and again. "We should go inside now," Amy said gently, "the priest is going to start soon, and you're up at the front pew." Mick nodded, letting her lead him up the steps, her arm lightly draped around his shoulders. As they entered the church, he noticed again the glowing light streaming through the windows, bathing the pews in soft radiance. The architecture felt timeless, the hundred-foot span of the pews leading to the pulpit, where the priest waited patiently.

Inside, the church was both familiar and foreign to him, a place of ritual he no longer belonged to but could mimic participation in. He knew the funeral would conclude with his mother's casket being taken to the cemetery, to rest in her final place. Father Jefferson began his oration, a graceful tribute that touched on his mother's kindness, her hard work, and her love for family and community. His voice was soothing, and those seated around Mick were visibly moved, some dabbing at their eyes with tissues. Mick looked around, his gaze lingering on Amy as she listened, her attention fully on the priest. He wondered if she had ever thought of him in any way other than as Sara's son. The idea intrigued him; she was divorced now, after all, and her beauty was as striking as ever.

As the service ended, Mick slipped outside to his car, watching as others piled into their vehicles, following the hearse and the police cars to the cemetery. He drove alone, his thoughts dark and tangled, isolated in his vehicle. At the burial site, people gathered around the open grave. As the casket was lowered, he noticed a short man in a dark suit and bowler hat standing about a hundred yards away, simply observing. Mick didn't recognize him, but the man's stillness, his quiet presence, was unnerving.

Back at the church for the reception, Mick saw Amy and some of his mother's friends moving inside. He wasn't hungry, so he wandered downstairs, following the murmur of voices in the kitchen, where people were helping themselves to coffee, sandwiches, and cake. He thanked Father Jefferson for his words, shaking the man's hand as the priest laid a comforting hand on his shoulder.

"Your mother was a remarkable woman, Mick," Father Jefferson said. "I did some research into your family while preparing my speech. Good, honest people, farmers doing their best to feed those around them. I never found a blemish in her character. She gave so much of herself and gave us you."

Mick forced a faint smile as he watched Priest Jefferson remove his hands from his shoulders, the priest's gentle yet firm touch lingering like a last tether to his fading innocence. "If only you knew," Mick thought, a silent murmur of the chaos within him. Priest Jefferson's words, though well-intentioned, struck him as almost ironic.

"Mick, make sure to grab some food," Jefferson encouraged, his voice warm. "You'll be needing to cook for yourself soon, I imagine."

Mick nodded, letting out a hollow laugh. "It's one of my favorite hobbies," he replied, feigning a casual ease he didn't feel. "I'm no master chef yet, but soon enough, I'll be the best cook around."

They both laughed, though only one of them meant it. As the priest moved on to speak with other mourners, Mick glanced across the room at his cousins, nine of them standing in a loose circle, eating quietly. These were relatives he'd barely known, faces that blurred together in his memory. As he walked over to them, he paused by a stained-glass window depicting Jesus with rays of light cascading down to his followers.

Mick's gaze lingered on the image, transfixed by the serenity in Jesus' expression. The stained glass was hypnotic, the deep blues and vivid reds, the light shining through in shimmering beams that seemed to breathe life into the figure's outstretched arms. For a fleeting moment, he almost wanted to believe in something as grand as salvation.

"With everything I've seen, why can't I see God?" he mused bitterly, his mind flashing back to his encounter with the Devil. He thought of that moment, the blade in his hand, the Devil's eyes watching him as he carved into flesh. He'd half-expected it to be an illusion, yet the wound had healed right before him, confirming the terrifying reality of his adversary. "If the Devil's real… then where's God?"

Mick shook himself from his reverie and finally joined his cousins. Their eyes turned toward him with somber expressions, but Drew, one of the few cousins Mick vaguely remembered, stepped forward, his face softening into a warm smile.

"No problem, Mick," Drew said. "Your dad was a good man, and he was lucky to find your mom. We'd be here any time." He hesitated, then added, "Are you gonna be okay, Mick? Just you in that big house now?"

Mick swallowed, forcing himself to maintain the charade. "Yeah, I'll be fine. Thank you all for being here. Really." He gestured toward the table laden with food. "There's plenty left, help yourselves."

Drew gave him a reassuring clap on the shoulder. "Take it easy, Mick," he said before the cousins drifted back to their conversation.

Mick turned away, his eyes scanning the room until he found his mother's friends, gathered in a similar circle on the opposite side. Their faces were etched with concern, and as he approached, Sheila, one of the older women, spoke up.

"We're doing fine, Mick," she said softly, her eyes glistening. "We're just worried about you."

Amy, standing beside her, reached out, placing a gentle hand on Mick's shoulder. "Yeah, Mick, are you going to be okay?"

The warmth of her touch seeped into his skin, surprising him. In his mind, he tried to shake off the cemetery, the tightness that had held his body like a vice during the burial. He managed a small, lopsided smile. "I'll be okay. Told Father Jefferson I'd better start learning to cook for myself now," he said, though the thought felt absurdly foreign. In reality, he'd been living off drive-thru meals and leftovers, his mother's home-cooked meals just a distant memory.

Amy's hand lingered, and she tilted her head, offering him a sympathetic smile. "How long will you be at Dunwood?"

"Until the end of the year," he replied. "Associates degree. After that, who knows? Maybe I'll go for a bachelor's, maybe I'll just start working."

Sheila's voice chimed in. "If you need anything, you know where to find us."

The funeral was winding down; volunteers from the church had already started clearing tables and stacking chairs. Mick exchanged brief, obligatory goodbyes with those who approached him, offering his thanks for their support. When Father Jefferson appeared again, his gentle eyes showed nothing but kindness.

"Mick, it's time for you to go home, get back to your life," Jefferson said, his words carrying a weight that Mick didn't fully understand.

"Yeah… there are some things that need doing."

As Mick walked out to the parking lot, he noticed Amy lingering by her car, her back leaning casually against it as she watched him approach. A flicker of something stirred in him, curiosity, maybe even hope. "Was she waiting for me?" he wondered, barely allowing himself to indulge the thought.

Amy straightened, her face softening as he drew near. "I'm so sorry, Mick," she said, her voice full of genuine sorrow. "It was way too soon for Sara to go." She wrapped her arms around him in a hug, her embrace surprisingly tender, grounding him for a moment in a way he hadn't anticipated. "If you need anything… anything at all, just call me. I'll be there."

"I'll remember that, Amy. Thank you."

She hugged him again, her warmth lingering as she pulled away and returned to her car. As she drove off, she cast one last glance back, a small, fleeting smile playing on her lips.

Watching her go, Mick felt a strange mixture of bitterness and attraction. He thought of all the younger women in his life who treated him with polite indifference, of Melissa, *well she just wanted to fuck*. Melissa and her shallow promises that had ended as quickly as they'd begun. He considered Amy, near sixty, but still attractive, the lines of age softened by a timeless charm. Maybe, he thought with a wry smile, she was his last chance to feel something real, to connect with someone beyond a fleeting embrace.

15

The Dark Descent

The months since Sara's death had settled over Mick like a heavy fog, blanketing his days in a dull routine. Every morning, he would drag himself to class, then retreat to the library, only to return to the hollow silence of his inherited house. He often found himself wandering from room to room, stopping occasionally to study the worn furniture and old family artifacts, each item a faint echo of the life that once animated this space.

The house, vast and cold, loomed as a daily reminder of his isolation. His mother had left him a comfortable sum of money, enough to keep him afloat for a long while, but Mick felt the weight of it more than its worth. He could sell it all, most of the furniture, the dusty memorabilia, but the thought of a garage sale always met a strange resistance in his mind. Maybe it was laziness, or maybe he didn't want to feel the finality of strangers picking over his parents' belongings. The lawyers assured him the insurance payment would come through soon, promising it would be more than enough to make him "quite happy." But happiness seemed like an elusive, foreign concept.

Late one Friday night, Mick found himself in front of his bathroom mirror, studying his reflection. Naked and silent, he stared into his own eyes, a strange emptiness reflecting back at him. The silence in his mind was disturbing, devoid of any real remorse, empathy, or warmth. He had always sensed something in himself, a darkness he didn't fully understand, something that had grown over the years, yet he didn't confront it. He didn't have to. The question, "Why?" echoed through his mind, but it was as if the answer stared back at him, unspoken but undeniable, right there in his own eyes.

The water ran cold over his hands as he splashed it on his face, snapping himself out of the trance. Drying his face with a towel, he wandered into his room, put on a pair of black shorts, and booted up his computer. He spent the next few hours scanning maps of nearby towns, his mind working through plans that surfaced as naturally as breathing.

"If I'm careful," he murmured, "I'll manage to pull this off without a hitch."

The thought was calculated, chillingly pragmatic. He weighed his options, knowing that impulsive behavior would only end in disaster. Highway restrooms were too risky now, public awareness had spread with recent news stories about missing women. No, he needed a new plan, something away from prying eyes, somewhere where people wouldn't be on high alert.

A solution materialized in his mind as he zoomed in on a map of Clanton, a small city about 220 miles away, Wal-Mart on Highway 55. A superstore on the edge of town with a sprawling parking lot, and on a Saturday night, there would be fewer people after closing. Perfect.

The next morning, Mick left before dawn, stopping only to fill up at a gas station, paying carefully at the pump to avoid unnecessary human interaction. His black attire, dark clothes, rubber gloves, and the essentials he'd packed the night before, made him feel like a shadow. Four hours later, he pulled into Clanton, his heart pounding with an unfamiliar rhythm as he parked at the far edge of the Wal-Mart lot, far enough away to go unnoticed but close enough to watch the entrance.

He settled into a rhythm, snacking on a sandwich as he surveyed the people trickling in and out of the store. His binoculars provided a closer look, letting him study the faces and mannerisms of each woman who passed through the automatic doors. Hours melted away, each tick of the clock heightening his anticipation. By 9 p.m., the lot had emptied to a manageable number, the rows of parked cars thinning until only a handful remained. Mick's pulse quickened as he realized the moment was closing in.

A woman, alone, exited the store, pushing a cart laden with groceries. She was red-haired, dressed in a casual blouse and jeans, her face serene as she navigated the rows. Mick's car rumbled to life as he discreetly followed her, circling around to approach from an adjacent aisle. She parked her cart and began to load bags into her trunk, the stillness of the empty lot amplifying every sound.

He stepped out of the car, hands steady, his grip tight around the weighted metal ball in his pocket. The woman glanced up, likely expecting to see a harmless passerby, but her eyes widened as she noticed the intensity in his expression. A tremor of fear flashed across her face.

"Can I help you?" Her voice broke, cut short as Mick closed the distance with a swift, practiced strike to her head. She stumbled, her hands fumbling in an attempt to defend herself, but Mick's grip was relentless. He dragged her, dazed, to the backseat, where he snapped on a pair of handcuffs.

"Redhead...perfect," Mick muttered under his breath as he slipped back into the driver's seat, heart racing from the thrill that still lingered. He stole a quick glance in the rearview mirror, where he caught sight of a child, no older than ten, standing alone in the dim parking lot, too far away to understand but close enough to possibly have seen something.

As he started the engine and eased out of the parking lot, he couldn't help but wonder. Did the kid see anything? Did he see Mick strike the girl, only seconds before? He kept his eyes on the road, forcing himself to drive at a steady, controlled speed, but he couldn't shake the lingering anxiety. He pushed the thought away, leaving the Walmart lights behind him as he merged onto the empty highway.

The hum of the engine and the smooth rhythm of the tires on the road brought him a sense of calm, a dark sort of tranquility that took the edge off his nerves. From the back seat, his captive let out a faint moan, pulling his attention back to the present. It was the same twisted feeling he knew well, the thrill that whispered to him, urging him toward the edge, urging him to surrender to that quiet, sinister pull.

16

The Abyss Stares Back

Mick sat in the dark silence of his room, the clock hands edging past midnight, the only sound the subtle whirring of the fan. Outside, the quiet was broken only by the chirping of crickets, their song weaving a hypnotic rhythm that merged with the stillness. Mick leaned his forehead against the cold glass of his bedroom window, looking out into the blackness, seeing not the empty street but something else, something far more twisted.

His thoughts drifted to his last victim, Iris Adams. She was supposed to be just another face, another conquest, but she lingered, her image burned into his mind. He'd felt something raw and thrilling while overpowering her, a sensation that now unsettled him. She had fought back, a resilience that most of his previous targets hadn't shown. Her screams had left an impression, not of guilt, but of a lingering curiosity, a need to explore this territory further, to refine his process.

Mick ran a hand through his dark hair and sat at his desk, reaching for his small, worn notebook. He turned to the last page, where he meticulously kept track of each victim's appearance, marking them with single words: "Blonde," "Brunette," "Blonde." With Iris, he added "Redhead." The ink was barely dry before he felt the tug of anticipation, the pull that had become both his driving force and his curse.

His thoughts veered to the practicalities. Disposal was always a chore, the burning, the chiseling, the endless hammering. Each time, the cleanup felt like drudgery, like he was clocking into some grotesque night shift. Yet there was satisfaction in the routine, in the way each ritual erased any trace of his deeds. But now, he had a new complication. A ten-year-old boy had seen him near the scene. The child likely wouldn't remember much, but he'd noted a few details: the dark red car, Mick's build, his height.

"A dark red car," Mick muttered, frowning. There were thousands like it, but it was still a risk. He'd need to dispose of it, bury it, perhaps. Pay cash for another. Every choice added a new layer to his already complex web of lies and secrecy.

The heavy stillness was broken by an unexpected chime. Mick froze, his eyes darting to the clock, 12:30 a.m., tension thickening in his veins. No one ever visited him, especially at this hour.

A flash of irritation crossed his face. Who could be so bold, or so foolish, to disturb him now?

Finally, he moved, each step measured. He descended the stairs, the dim glow from the hall casting long shadows. He reached the door and grasped the knob, pausing for just a moment. He could have looked through the peephole, but the thrill of the unknown was too strong.

Mick opened the door to reveal Amy, her eyes glazed, her body swaying slightly. She was wrapped in a pink dress that seemed to cling to her every curve, and he could smell the sharp scent of alcohol that clung to her.

"Hi, Mick…can I come in?" Her voice was a whisper, her words slurring slightly as she leaned against the doorframe. "I… I miss Sara. I just wanted to talk."

Mick's mind raced. He hadn't seen Amy in weeks. His mother's old friend, and a divorcee who had known Mick since he was a child. Her ex-husband was a salesman living in Europe. Now, here she was, vulnerable, her defenses down, looking to him for comfort in a way that felt almost too serendipitous.

"Sure, Amy. Come on in," Mick replied smoothly, stepping aside to let her enter. His heart began to thump with a mixture of anticipation and something darker, something he tried to bury every time it reared its head.

As she stumbled through the door, Mick caught a glimpse of her cleavage, accentuated by the plunging neckline of her dress. He felt a stirring he hadn't anticipated, his usual cold detachment fracturing under a different kind of hunger. This was his mother's friend, a woman he'd known for years, yet he could feel his instincts sharpening, his predatory side quietly awakening.

"Have you been drinking, Amy?" Mick asked, trying to keep his voice steady.

"Just a little," she murmured, shrugging off her coat and letting it fall to the floor. Mick's gaze followed her as she moved, her body swaying with a languid, almost hypnotic rhythm. "I... I just miss Sara so much. We used to go everywhere together. I feel so... lonely."

Loneliness. Mick knew the feeling well, but for him, it was a different kind of solitude, one that he wore like a second skin, that fed his darker cravings. He studied Amy with a growing fascination. Her vulnerability made her different, unlike the carefully selected victims he usually pursued. She had come to him willingly, almost as if she'd known what he truly was.

As if on cue, Amy stepped closer, her pink dress slipping slightly off her shoulder, revealing smooth skin beneath. Mick felt his restraint slipping, the thin barrier between his two worlds beginning to crumble. He reached out, his hand resting on her shoulder, feeling her warmth through his fingertips. She looked up at him with heavy-lidded eyes, her breath hitching as he moved closer.

"I'm... lonely, Mick," she whispered, her voice barely audible.

Without a word, he slid his hand down her arm, tracing the lines of her body as she closed her eyes and leaned into his touch. In that moment, he was lost, the boundaries he had so carefully constructed around his life dissolving into something primal, something unrestrained.

Mick grabbed her wrist and yanked her into Mom's bedroom. Thankfully, he hadn't yet sold her things. The bed, still there, waited for them both as he threw her onto it.

Mick stripped off her clothes, and their bodies moved and glided into each other through several different positions. Each time he glanced at her face, her eyes remained closed. He made love to her with desire and passion that reverberated off the walls. She moaned loudly in his ear with every thrust, spanks, and bite she received. She gave in to him, allowing Mick to have her as he pleased. His shaft stood erect and wet, and the junction of her thighs remained open, her legs over his shoulders as her body jerked with every shot. "More lust than romance," he thought.

After they were finished, Mick lay there in a haze, caught between sleep and wakefulness. He glanced at the clock, 4:30 a.m. Slowly, he pulled himself out of bed and made his way upstairs to use the bathroom. When he returned, he stood silently above Amy, watching her sleep soundly. Naked, except for the black rubber gloves on his hands, he absentmindedly rolled his metal ball from one hand to the other.

A dark thought crossed his mind. *"I can't do it."* He wrestled with the impulse. *"If I killed her, it would be like killing myself. The cops would catch me in an instant."* His heart raced, but his mind fought to regain control. *"Control the impulse."*

With a frustrated sigh, Mick turned and trudged back upstairs. *"Maybe she'll be gone by morning,"* he thought as he crawled back into bed, trying to shut out the unsettling thoughts that clouded his mind.

17

Leinholder's Legacy

Mick sat silently, gazing out the tall windows of the insurance office on a crisp Thursday morning. The office had an air of refined efficiency, with secretaries in smart attire bustling about, maintaining the polished professional vibe. The walls were lined with muted art pieces, the kind meant to invoke calmness and authority, and Mick couldn't help but feel small in the sterile, business-like environment. This wasn't his world, but he was here for a reason, waiting for a transaction that felt surreal, receiving the insurance payout for his mother's life.

For years, he'd known his mom kept a policy in his name. She'd mentioned it once or twice, especially after his dad passed, but Mick had never given it much thought, never asked for details or specifics. It was only now, after her passing, that he understood the weight of it, the tangible evidence of her love and planning, even in her absence. The whole thing seemed straightforward enough: he'd go through some paperwork, give them his account information, and the money would be wired over. He wasn't sure what to expect from the process, but he hoped for it to be simple and fast. He wasn't one for drawn-out conversations or emotional overtures, not now, not ever.

Two men in soft blue suits entered the room, giving polite nods to the secretaries as they moved through the office. Mick's mind wandered as he waited, occasionally locking eyes with one of the secretaries who glanced at him with quiet curiosity, as if she could sense he was a stranger in this polished world. His thoughts drifted to the weekend and the work waiting at home. He'd planned a garage sale to clear out his mother's things, her materials, fabrics, and endless supplies of textiles. She'd had an eye for beauty and quality, and it showed in the careful selections she'd kept over the years. But Mick didn't need them, and he certainly didn't need the memories they would evoke. It wasn't about the money; he was in it to make space, to rid himself of the past in physical form, piece by piece. Anything left unsold, he'd give away for free, just to make sure nothing lingered.

Finally, one of the men approached him, extending a hand. "Hi Mick, I'm Joel Miller. I handled your mom's case after your father passed," he said, his tone heavy with sympathy. "I'm truly sorry for your loss. She was a wonderful lady, taken too soon."

Mick shook his hand firmly, offering a short, "Thanks, Joel." Joel gave him a reassuring nod, diving straight into business. "Let's keep this quick. We'll just need a few signatures, and then we can process everything electronically. You won't get a physical check; we'll deposit the funds directly into your checking account. That work for you?"

"Yes," Mick replied. "When it comes to business, I like things done ASAP."

The two men guided him into a glass-walled office, where a neat stack of papers awaited. Mick's hand tightened around the pen as he worked through the documents, confirming his identity, verifying his mother's relationship to him, and signing off on her last gift to him. A mixture of grief and relief settled over him as he scrawled his name across the final line. When he finished, he looked at Joel, the weight of the moment pressing down on him.

"How much?" Mick asked, his voice barely above a whisper.

Joel offered him a solemn smile. "Half a million, Mick. Your mom took care of things well."

The numbers echoed in Mick's mind as he walked out of the office, a strange satisfaction settling over him. Half a million, plus the $800,000 his mother had saved over the years. Altogether, $1.3 million, a considerable sum, a lasting legacy from his mother. "Thanks, Mom," he thought, glancing upward as he unlocked his car. The gratitude was fleeting, however, as his thoughts shifted back to the challenges looming on the horizon. He had bigger issues, ones money couldn't so easily fix.

Mick's red car was part of a mess he wanted to forget, an anchor to memories he couldn't shake. His involvement in a mishap in Clanton City lingered like a shadow, dark and invasive. Some kid had seen his car; he was sure of it. The boy's eyes had widened as Mick had driven past, catching a glimpse just in time. Mick's mind spiraled, replaying the scene: the woman, the hurried movement, the impulse that had driven him to act without thinking. He had to clear his tracks. After the garage sale, he decided, he'd ditch the red car, bury it in his past, and buy a new one, paying in cash to keep it clean. For now, he'd keep it in the garage, hidden from prying eyes.

That afternoon, he drove to Star One Pawn, his mother's jewelry carefully packed in his gym bag beside him. She had amassed an impressive collection over the years: gold, diamonds, pearls, stones of every color. Each piece carried a memory, a significance he couldn't quite grasp. He wasn't sentimental about jewelry, but he knew its worth, and he needed to turn it into cash. The pawn shop's neon sign flickered against the dull street, a garish beacon in the overcast afternoon.

Inside, the shop was a stark contrast to the polished offices he'd just left. Glass counters held a chaotic assortment of goods, watches, rings, necklaces, all begging for a second life. The man behind the counter, with his slicked-back hair and a smirk that could slice glass, gave Mick a once-over.

"Afternoon," the salesman greeted, his tone oozing practiced charm. "What've you got for me?"

Mick didn't like the look of him, but he kept his disdain hidden, forcing a tight smile. "I've got some jewelry I'd like to sell."

The man's eyes lit up, and he motioned for Mick to place the items on the counter. Mick carefully set down several rings, necklaces, and bracelets, watching the salesman's reaction as he eyed the pieces with a discerning gaze. "All real," Mick assured him. "Diamonds, gold, silver, nothing fake here."

The salesman leaned over, pulling out a magnifying glass, his face a mask of intent concentration as he inspected each piece. "God damn," he muttered. "These look good... real good. Tell me, kid, where'd you come across these?"

Mick bristled at the question, his fists clenching unconsciously. "They belonged to a relative. They're mine now."

The salesman shrugged, unimpressed by Mick's defensiveness. "No need to get worked up. Just asking." He set a ring back on the counter, glancing at Mick with an appraising look. "How many pieces are we talking here?"

Mick recited the inventory without hesitation. "Fifteen rings, twenty-four necklaces, and a bunch of earrings."

The salesman nodded, whistling low. "That's quite the haul. They all look good, but if I'm buying this many, I'll need a bit more information. Age, origin... it'll take some time to come up with a proper price."

Mick nodded reluctantly. "Fine. You can take photos. I'll leave one or two pieces with you, so you can verify whatever you need. I'm not in a rush."

The man flashed a satisfied smile. "Works for me. Let's get to it, then." He retrieved his phone and began snapping pictures, adjusting the angle and lighting to capture each gem's brilliance. Mick watched him closely, a sense of distaste building with every click. He could sense the greed in the man's eyes, the way he lingered over the more valuable pieces.

When they were done, Mick gathered up the remaining jewelry, careful not to let his disdain show. They exchanged numbers, the tension palpable.

As Mick was heading toward the exit, he asked, "Hey... do you have any daughters?"

"What?" asked the salesman, looking puzzled.

"Never mind," Mick replied, brushing off the question.

The rest of that Thursday, Mick spent cleaning out his garage as best he could, moving some tools to his downstairs office, which was packed with storage boxes. He crafted a few garage sale signs to post around the neighborhood, deciding to place them at busier intersections for visibility. As he drove back, hunger struck, so he stopped by to grab some ingredients, then fired up the grill to prepare marinated chicken breasts and sliced potatoes. While waiting for the grill to heat up, he switched on the TV.

Just in time, the news was covering the story of Iris Adams, a woman missing for over a week. Authorities suspected her disappearance might be connected to a string of recent abductions in the area. They showed her picture and mentioned she'd last been seen near a Walmart.

Mick switched off the TV, feeling a sudden wave of frustration. He muttered to himself, "Each time... each time it slips away. I clean up, dispose of, and scatter every trace. Dumpsters, landfills… they'd need a miracle to find anything." He paused, lost in thought. "Except… that kid…"

Meanwhile, across town, Alice Reed was preparing dinner. Divorced for two years, she'd been raising her two boys on her own. As she stirred the pot, her attention shifted to the news story about Iris Adams. She realized she and her kids had been at that Walmart around the same time as the reported abduction.

"Boys, it's dinner time!" she called out. Her sons, Rick and Ray, dashed in from the backyard, playfully nudging each other. "Wash up and get to the table," she reminded them. As they sat down to plates of chicken, rice, and green beans, Alice found herself revisiting that day. Could there have been something she missed?

"Hey, Rick, Ray," she began. "Remember when we were at Walmart last week?"

"Yeah," Rick replied through a mouthful of food.

"Did you see anything… unusual?" she asked, carefully.

Rick looked thoughtful. "Well… there were two people, kind of playing tag or something," he said. "A guy was chasing a girl, and then he threw something at her. Maybe a tennis ball?"

"Why didn't you tell me this before?" Alice asked, concerned.

Rick hesitated, his expression turning uneasy. "This kid at school, Scott, he said if I told on anyone again, I'd get it bad… that 'rats don't last long,'" he said, his voice wavering.

Alice reached over, hugging him gently. "That's just bullying, Rick. You're safe with me. But this is serious; what happened at Walmart is different. Can you remember what the man looked like?"

Rick sniffled. "He was white… wearing a black shirt and dark pants. After he hit her, he took her behind his car and drove off. His car was red."

Alice's face paled. "Thank you, sweetheart," she whispered.

Meanwhile, back at Mick's house, he finished his meal and returned to organizing items for the sale. He tossed aside anything he didn't need, mentally noting that he'd still have to photograph the larger furniture pieces for Facebook Marketplace. Sighing, he thought about the hassle of dealing with his car, which could potentially attract attention if anyone remembered it.

Later that evening, his doorbell rang. "I think I know who that is," he muttered, heading to open the door.

"Hi, Mick," Amy greeted him, holding a six-pack with three beers left.

"Hey, I thought you only went out on weekends?" Mick replied, surprised.

"Oh, lately every day feels like a weekend," she laughed, offering him a beer. "Want one?"

"Sure," Mick accepted.

Amy glanced around. "Looks like you're gearing up for a garage sale. Getting rid of some stuff?"

"Yeah, don't need it," he replied. "Want any jewelry? Haven't tossed that yet."

She shook her head. "Got plenty of my own." They stood close, almost sharing the same space, a strange tension hanging between them.

As she moved closer, he could sense her intentions, but something in him remained detached, his mind drifting to thoughts that she couldn't fulfill.

Mick could tell Amy had been drinking, though not as much as last time. Standing close, they looked at each other with a familiarity that had grown over time.

"I've been a bit naughty, haven't I?" Amy murmured, a playful gleam in her eyes. "It's like I came over just to take my best friend's son, and have him give me...pleasure."

Mick gave a faint smile, meeting her gaze. "Maybe it's a little more than just flirting," he replied. "But we're both here, and... I think we're both drawn to it. You are an attractive woman, but yes… you are naughty. And for that, you're gonna get a good spanking before I fuck you."

As they moved closer, Mick noticed something he hadn't before: a certain vulnerability beneath her words and laughter. While she seemed to seek comfort or thrill, he knew that whatever they shared didn't fully satisfy the deeper needs they each carried.

The more and more I see of her, the more cracks she has. She wants pleasure, sure, no problem, but my abstract desire and lust…that she cannot fulfill, he thought.

Mick placed his hands gently on her shoulders, turning her toward him. Drawing her close, he let his arms rest around her, one on her throat, and the other to put her hands to her back, guiding her softly as they began to move toward his mom's bedroom.

Her whisper was barely audible, a quiet, "Oh yes…yes," as they continued forward, wrapped in the moment.

18

An Unsettling Morning

Mick squinted at his phone's glowing screen, 9:34 a.m. He shook off the lingering haze of sleep, a bit surprised to find himself alone again. Amy had her habit, and he was beginning to anticipate it. Her visits had become routine: she'd come by, enjoy her moments, and then vanish by morning, leaving only faint traces behind. She'd head out without a word, leaving him to wake in the stillness, while she used his mother's old bedroom.

For Mick, this arrangement worked. "Maybe I won't sell Mom's bed after all," he mused, pulling himself out of bed.

The morning light seeped through his blinds as he settled at his desk, opening up his laptop. He had plenty of work to catch up on, particularly his assignments from Dunwood Community College. Most of the day slipped by in the quiet hum of his computer, and Mick realized, with some satisfaction, that he was close to wrapping up his associate degree. His thoughts drifted momentarily, while the bachelor's program might have to wait, he knew he could return whenever he was ready.

By 3:00 p.m., Mick decided it was time for a break. He headed out to a large farm and sporting goods store to buy a new cover for his car. He wanted something sizable, heavy enough to keep it fully concealed. After a bit of searching, he settled on a large gray cover, the right fit to mask any sign of the car beneath.

"Even if it's painted over someday, there'd always be traces of the old color beneath the surface," Mick thought. For now, he'd keep it tucked away in the garage, its bright red hidden from prying eyes.

As the afternoon waned, Mick's sense of unease lingered, but he shook it off. At 5:30, he decided on something simple for dinner, burgers. He considered switching on the news while he ate, but the idea soured on him. News broadcasts, with their endless pleas for witness information and talk of crime in the community, felt increasingly repetitive. It had been a week since the latest disappearance, yet Mick still wondered if that kid he'd seen had forgotten anything from that day.

***

Across town, the atmosphere at Clanton Police Station was tense but purposeful. Alice Reed sat anxiously in the lobby with her son, Rick. She had told the school that Rick wasn't feeling well today. The truth, though, was that Rick had witnessed something troubling, something he didn't fully understand, and she knew he needed to share it with the authorities.

Approaching the front desk, Alice caught the attention of an officer who looked up from his paperwork.

"How can I help you, ma'am?"

"I need to speak with someone about the woman who went missing from the Walmart parking lot last week," Alice replied, her voice steady.

The officer's expression shifted as he glanced over at her and then down to young Rick, who stood by her side. "You have information on that case?"

Alice nodded. "My son Rick saw what happened."

The officer gestured toward a row of chairs against the wall. "Wait over there for a moment. I'll get Detective Bennet. He'll want to talk to you both."

They had barely settled into their seats before Detective Dick Bennet, a bearded man in a neatly pressed gray suit, approached with a purposeful stride. He introduced himself, then turned to Rick with a warm, reassuring smile.

"Hi, Rick. How are you doing today?"

Rick looked up at him, nerves visible but steady. "I'm fine, sir."

"So, you saw something happen last week? Can you tell me about it?" Bennet asked, his tone gentle.

Rick nodded, glancing at his mom for encouragement. "Yes, sir. I saw a man hit a lady and then put her in a car."

Detective Bennet's gaze shifted from Rick to Alice. "Thank you for bringing him in, Alice. Let's go to one of our offices where we can talk more privately, maybe even grab you both a quick breakfast."

In a small office down the hall, with a chalkboard on the wall and windows letting in the mid-morning light, they took a seat. Bennet stepped out briefly, instructing his secretary to bring bagels and juice for their guests. Then, he headed back to his desk and picked up the phone, dialing Detective Andrew Taylor, the lead on the investigation.

Detective Taylor answered promptly. "Taylor here."

"Morning, Detective. This is Bennet over in Clanton. I think we've got a break on the Iris Adams case. A kid and his mom just came in, young Rick here saw Iris being struck and then taken in a car," Bennet said, his voice calm but charged with anticipation.

Taylor let out a long breath, his tension easing slightly. "Exactly what we needed to move forward. How many witnesses did you say?"

"Just one. The boy saw it firsthand," Bennet replied. "I figured you'd want to speak with him personally."

Taylor glanced at his watch. "I can be there by 2:00 p.m. How old is the boy?"

"He's around ten, maybe eleven. Sharp kid. I'll keep him and his mom here until you arrive."

After the call, Bennet returned to the office to update Alice and Rick. "Detective Taylor will be here by 1:00 to speak with you both. If you'd like, you're welcome to stay in here until he arrives."

Andrew Taylor arrived at the Clanton Police Department at precisely 1:27 p.m. He adjusted his jacket as he walked in and asked for Detective Bennet at the front desk.

"Good afternoon, sir. I'm Detective Andrew Taylor," he greeted when Bennet appeared.

"Hello. Just call me Dick," Bennet replied, extending a hand. "The witnesses are in an office toward the back. The boy's name is Rick, and his mother is Alice. They were leaving Walmart right when Iris was abducted, and Rick says he saw it happen." Bennet spoke in a low voice as they neared the office door.

"Thank you, Dick," said Andrew, bracing himself.

"Good luck," Bennet replied with a slight nod.

Andrew stepped inside, where Alice and Rick sat waiting. "Hi, Alice," he greeted, taking a seat opposite them. "And you must be Rick."

"Yep, that's me," Rick answered, with a small smile.

Alice looked encouragingly at her son. "Tell the detective everything you saw, Rick."

Andrew pulled out a pen and notebook, ready to capture every detail. Rick took a breath before starting. "Me and Ray, my brother, were coming out of Walmart, kinda playing tag. I thought these two other people were playing tag too, because the guy was going after the girl. But then... he hit her. He hit her with something instead of tagging her, then put her in his car and drove off."

Andrew leaned forward slightly, keeping his tone gentle. "Rick, can you tell me what the guy looked like? Try to stretch your memory as best as you can."

Rick thought for a moment. "He had brown hair, but he was white. I couldn't see his face well, the sun was setting, and they were kinda far away."

"Do you remember his height?" Andrew probed, hoping for anything more specific.

Rick's face scrunched as he tried to recall. "He wasn't really tall, but not short either. About six feet, maybe?"

Andrew nodded. "Was there anything else you remember? You said he drove off after putting her in the car?"

"Yeah, he just drove off," Rick confirmed.

"Did you happen to see the license plate?" Andrew asked, holding his breath.

Rick shook his head. "No… I know you're supposed to have one on the car, but I didn't look at it."

Andrew pressed a little further. "Plates usually have letters and numbers. Did you catch any of them?"

Rick frowned, shaking his head again. "Nope. That's it."

Andrew sighed inwardly but kept his expression calm. "Thank you, Rick. You've been very helpful." He looked at Alice. "Alice, we'll document everything and may need you to sign some forms to confirm his statement."

Alice nodded. "I saw something about a reward on TV… Will this lead to that $50,000 they're offering?"

Andrew leaned back. "Only if it helps us find Iris or leads to an arrest," he explained.

Alice gave a hopeful nod. "Okay."

***

Meanwhile, Mick was at home, staring into his bathroom mirror, fighting an internal struggle. Midnight had come and gone, but sleep was far from his mind. Instead, his eyes lingered on his reflection, his thoughts churning with an intensity that bordered on dread.

"My first kills," he muttered, "had such satisfaction, a sense of fulfillment. It was nostalgic in a strange way… but this time…" He paused, rubbing his temple as if to dispel the gnawing discomfort. "The fulfillment fades so quickly now. Anxiety's taking over. Instead of the emptiness I used to feel, I'm left with a gnawing fear."

Mick's eyes narrowed, his reflection feeling strangely foreign. "I must fulfill myself!" he whispered fiercely. "I used to be able to go months, but now... it's weeks. Days, even. If I let this weakness take hold, they'll catch me."

The moments ticked by, and finally, exhaustion seeped in. As he staggered to bed and closed his eyes, he found himself descending into a surreal, sinister dream.

In the darkness of his mind, Lucifer appeared, dressed impeccably in a three-piece suit and bowler hat. His thin mustache curled as he frowned, his eyes cold and penetrating as they bore into Mick. This was no figure of action or rage; Lucifer's power was in his words, each one like a blade.

Mick's dream shifted, and now he watched women skating on a smooth, black ice surface, each one performing daring spins and twirls as if trying to impress some unseen audience. They wore matching gray skirts and pristine white skates, their movements almost hypnotic, flowing in endless circles around each other. There were four of them, each lost in a performance that seemed to lack a true end.

One by one, the skaters continued their routine until the ice began to fracture. Slowly, cracks spidered beneath their feet, and with each spin, another piece of the ice gave way, and they began to disappear beneath the surface, one after the other. When all were gone, the ice closed over, smooth and reflective, as if nothing had happened.

Mick turned, his eyes meeting Lucifer's, whose sinister grin revealed a deep, twisted satisfaction. "Mick... where is my fifth skater?" Lucifer's voice was a low hiss, his laugh echoing in the blackness. "Where?"

Mick woke up, drenched in sweat, his heart pounding as the echoes of Lucifer's laughter faded into the silence of his empty room.

19

We're Close

Detective Andrew Taylor felt a familiar weight settle on his shoulders as he paused outside the interview room. He'd spoken with young Rick Reed three times that day, carefully pulling bits of information from the boy, but the kid's memory was scattered, and the details were slim. Each session felt like an uphill climb. Andrew could tell Rick was trying to be helpful, but he was just a kid, a kid caught in the whirlwind of witnessing something brutal. It pained Andrew that Rick hadn't managed to catch the license plate of the abductor's car. That single missed detail could have cracked the case wide open.

Andrew scratched his head in frustration, musing to himself, *I'm convinced this killer's from Ashland. I need to know if he had a history with Melissa, maybe a student, someone from the school, or an old flame? Anyone connected enough to drive him to this point. I know it's a long shot, but sometimes it's the smallest damn things that stitch together the truth.*

Andrew replayed the case details in his mind, feeling the weight of each missing woman pressing against his thoughts. Melissa had been the first, taken right from Ashland. A small town like that doesn't forget a missing face, especially not the first in a series. He was convinced the killer lived there at some point, possibly crossing paths with her. The second victim had disappeared thirty miles south, yanked from the parking lot of a bar. Her car was still parked right where she'd left it. By the third abduction, they were looking at eighty miles south. Then came the fourth, a full two hundred miles down the line, southward again, a pattern as clear as day, if you looked hard enough.

As he thought through the case again, an idea clicked. *This guy is calculated, strikes fast and clean. Stuns them, no blood, no scene. Something blunt, maybe iron knuckles. No, too light. Could be a metal rod, or even a cast-iron ball? Yeah, something compact and deadly.* He pulled out his phone and ran a quick search on impact weapons. *Something three to five inches across. Small, brutal, perfect for knocking someone out cold in one hit.*

His mind swirled with the image, a man, white, early twenties, six feet, brown hair, dressed all in black during the abductions, driving a red car. *Someone young enough to blend in, old enough to know what he's doing,* Andrew thought darkly. The profile matched half the damn town, but Andrew was betting his life this guy had crossed paths with Melissa, probably at Ashland High. *Doesn't matter why he's doing it,* Andrew told himself, *All that matters is stopping him before he gets away again.*

Across town, Priest Gary Brown sat hunched over his desk, scribbling ideas for his next sermon. He was aiming for something meaningful, yet easy for his congregation to grasp, a gentle narrative with a powerful punch. His mind moved through the puzzle pieces of his sermon, placing one next to the other, building an intricate tapestry of spiritual guidance. Lost in thought, he was startled when Priest Stewart walked in, all smiles.

"Ah, Gary, hard at work, I see!" Stewart said, leaning against the doorframe.

Gary looked up, smiling back. "Not quite writing yet. I'm treating it like a puzzle, making sure all the pieces are in place before putting anything down on paper."

"Ah, so, organized as ever," Stewart said, chuckling.

"Exactly," Gary replied.

Stewart's smile widened. "You know, your last two sermons have really struck a chord. The higher-ups, the… 'elites,' as you might call them, are impressed. They're talking about bringing you into some of these big mental health initiatives, combining theology and psychology. Jealous, even."

Gary chuckled softly. "There's nothing to be jealous of, David. I find the work stimulating, but it's not like I'm trying to reinvent the church."

Stewart gave a knowing nod. "True, true. Plenty of priests have done this before. But it's a unique chance to meet new minds, collaborate on theories, though, I doubt it'll change how we deal with, let's say, confessions."

Gary looked thoughtful. "Confession, huh? For criminal behavior?"

"Yes," Stewart said, a hint of caution in his voice. "You know the drill. Spiritual confessions can't be dragged into court. All we can do is guide the sinner to do what's right."

Gary looked down, his expression pensive. "Well... God does work in mysterious ways."

Stewart gave a solemn nod. "Yes, He does."

Elsewhere, Mick Enderson smirked as he readied for his garage sale. His car was hidden from view, deep in the backyard, concealed beneath a tarp. *Can't have anyone seeing the damn red paint,* he thought, shaking his head. He recalled the boy who'd seen him haul that girl, just as he'd struck her down. The image irritated him.

As he sold off junk, he kept glancing at the time. By afternoon, he planned to buy a used car he'd seen advertised, a gray Infiniti. *Cash only. No paper trail. Clean getaway.* He barely cared about the sale itself; money was secondary. All that mattered was ditching his red car. The kid saw it; that much was clear.

Last thing I need is some kid recognizing my damn car, he thought bitterly, tossing a cracked clock into a buyer's hands. Mick was ready to rid himself of anything, of anyone, who threatened his game.

Mick was hauling a scratched-up table out of his garage, arranging it to catch more eyes, when he felt a jolt. Someone was behind him.

"Hi Mick," a familiar voice sang out.

He spun around, heart hammering, to see Kim from Dunwood standing there, her bright smile a stark contrast to the gnawing anxiety simmering in his gut.

"Kim," he forced a smile. "What brings you all the way out here?"

"Not far from me at all," she said with a playful laugh. "Just hunting for some bargains. Dunwood doesn't exactly pay me a fortune." She giggled, and Mick noticed the way her eyes danced with warmth and ease. "Oh, and I'd love for you to meet my boyfriend!" she added, an unexpected glint in her eyes.

Mick's mind reeled, and his insides tightened with a sick, irrational jealousy. *Of course, she has a boyfriend,* he chided himself. *She's gorgeous, smart, who wouldn't be after her? Don't be an idiot.* But still, the thought of it made him clench his teeth. And yet, he knew he had to play nice.

She gestured to a man inspecting one of the rusting lawnmowers on display. "Daryl, come over here! This is Mick; we work together at Dunwood."

Daryl strolled over, extending a hand with a relaxed, friendly smile. "Hey, Mick. Got some good stuff here, I've actually been looking for a lawnmower."

Forcing a grin, Mick took his hand. "Take it for free, man. No charge."

Daryl laughed, surprised. "No way, I'll pay you something for it."

Mick shook his head quickly, shoving down the pang of resentment bubbling inside. "Nah, really. Take it as a gift."

"Wow, thanks, Mick!" Kim beamed at him, clearly thrilled by his gesture.

Forcing his face into a smile, he put his hand on Daryl's shoulder, guiding him over to the Expedition. They loaded the old mower into the back, and Daryl gave a casual wave as he closed the trunk. Mick watched them walk away, a fire brewing under his skin as he fixated on Kim's figure disappearing down the driveway. *Denial.*

As soon as they were out of sight, he let out a sharp breath and muttered, "Fuck."

The sight of Kim with someone else was more than enough to set him off-balance, but it was nothing compared to the other thoughts clawing at him. *Stay in control. Be smart.* He couldn't risk any more mistakes. There was still that witness, a young boy who had seen more than he should have. Mick didn't know if the kid had talked to anyone, but he couldn't afford to get careless. He just had to wait, let things cool down, cover his tracks. The car, his old red one…*Shit, what am I gonna do with that?*

Hours later, he slipped an envelope thick with cash into his waist bag, grabbed a crumpled address scrawled on a piece of paper, and headed out on his bike. The ride to Aaron's place was quick, and when he pulled up, his new car gleamed in the driveway, a sleek, gray Infiniti. Perfect.

Mick knocked on the door, and Aaron, a burly guy in his forties, answered with a polite nod. "Hey, you must be Curt," he greeted.

"That's right. And you're Aaron, right?" Mick answered smoothly.

Aaron led him over to the car. "Take a look. Runs like a charm. Only 60,000 miles on it."

Mick waved it off. "Nah, I trust you," he said, handing over the envelope, trying not to wince as he thought of the cash slipping out of his hands. "Besides, I know where you live."

Aaron chuckled, counting the money carefully, while Mick stashed his bike in the trunk.

"All here," Aaron said, smiling. He handed over the title and keys, and Mick felt a grim satisfaction bubbling up inside.

Later, when he got home, Mick backed his red car deep into the garage, draped a thick tarp over it, and parked the Infiniti outside in the driveway. He leaned against his bedroom wall, staring at the ceiling as he whispered to himself, "Wait, Let it simmer, The drive, the fire…it'll have to wait." A dark, almost peaceful calm washed over him as he recalled his last kill, the rush, the thrill of control.

20

The Case of Missing Threads

Detective Andrew Taylor sat at his desk, a dim light casting long shadows across the piles of paperwork scattered before him. The missing person case loomed heavily in his mind, each piece of evidence a fragment of an incomplete puzzle. Andrew leaned back in his chair, hands clasped behind his head, and mentally listed the pros and cons of their progress so far.

The best thing they had going was the series of commercials they had produced, hoping to jog someone's memory or unearth a witness to the crime. "If only Rick had gotten a better look," Andrew thought, frustration tightening his jaw. He whispered to himself, "A license plate number, even just a single letter or digit, anything could have been helpful." Rick had only caught a glimpse of the vehicle, and since he hadn't seen the abductor's face, Andrew doubted Rick could be reliable as a witness if the case ever went to trial.

Andrew's thoughts turned to Lieutenant Parker, whom he had assigned to chase down leads at several local schools. Parker was combing through graduation books and outdoor photos from the years surrounding Melissa's graduation. It was a long shot, but Andrew was convinced the killer might have been a peer, someone who graduated with Melissa or within a year of her.

Parker's task wasn't easy. Most of Melissa's former teachers had already been questioned, yet none had mentioned anything about a red car until recently. Parker had circled back, hoping fresh questioning might yield a different answer. Outdoors, the warm hum of the schoolyards and the murmur of teachers replaying their memories added to the sense of urgency. But it wasn't just the teachers. The students, Melissa's former classmates, posed another challenge. Two years had passed since her disappearance, and most had moved on, scattered across various colleges. Tracking them down was proving to be a daunting task, especially with the department's minimal budget.

Andrew stared at the map pinned to the wall, small pins marking locations tied to the case. His gut told him he was onto something, but the lack of concrete evidence weighed on him. "A young teacher? A tutor?" he wondered aloud, scribbling potential connections in the margins of his notebook. The suspect pool felt endless, over a hundred people could fit the vague description, and many of them were no longer even in town.

As the day wore on, Andrew stood and paced the length of his office. His thoughts churned. "Sometimes, you put in good work and find what you're looking for," he muttered, his voice heavy with both determination and weariness. "Other times, you need a stroke of luck." He couldn't shake the nagging thought that the abductor might already be far away, across state lines, maybe even repainting or destroying the red car that had briefly entered Rick's field of vision.

He sat back down, flipping through the stack of notes Lieutenant Parker had brought in. Andrew began drafting a list, names of students and staff who had been at the school during Melissa's time. "Find them," he thought, his pen moving furiously across the paper. "At least call them. Someone has to know something."

The room fell silent except for the scratching of his pen and the faint hum of the overhead light. Andrew paused, gripping the bridge of his nose. He closed his eyes, the weight of the case pressing down. "I wish I knew if the abductor even saw Rick," he murmured. "But I have to assume he did." His mind wandered back to the red car, its fleeting presence now the focal point of their investigation. Somewhere, someone was trying to erase that car from existence.

21

Fractured Masks

Mick sat at his desk, the glow of his laptop screen illuminating the otherwise dimly lit room. The final online submissions for his graduation at Dunwood had just been uploaded. For most students, the coming days would be filled with celebration, surrounded by family and friends. But not Mick.

"No family or friends," he muttered to himself, staring at the digital confirmation of his achievement. "What now? A job? Mom left me more money than I could ever need... and this house." His gaze flicked to the window, the manicured lawn beyond looking pristine under the pale moonlight.

A notification chimed on his phone, jolting him out of his thoughts.

Hello Mick, sorry about taking so long to get back to you. I've got the prices on the jewels you brought in. I'll be around most days except Sunday. Stop by, and we'll talk. – Cory Smith

Mick scowled. *Cory Smith. That guy's an asshole.* Still, he needed the money from the jewels. The thought of returning to Dunwood for another degree appealed to him; college life kept him busy and distracted. It offered structure.

***

Later, Mick showered and dressed, his clean Infiniti waiting in the driveway. The car was one of his few indulgences, sleek and meticulously maintained. As he drove to the campus, he couldn't help but think about how life seemed to shrink as time moved on.

He parked near the main building, the familiar sight of the library catching his eye. "Life is strange," he murmured. "Infinite possibilities reduced to routine and limitations. No excitement, no surprises."

Making his way to Kim's office, he rehearsed what he wanted to say. Kim had always been kind, professional, and patient with him. He knocked lightly on the door and saw her look up, signaling him to wait as she finished her phone call.

Kim. She was a vision in her pink blouse, her fiery red hair glowing under the fluorescent lights. He felt his heart quicken, but his mind whispered darker thoughts.

Could I… kill her? The notion was fleeting but insidious. *She's like all the others. Rejecting me without a word. If things were different… maybe she'd be mine.*

Kim finished her phone call, then gestured for Mick to sit.

"Hi, Kim," Mick said, his voice even but accompanied by a polite smile.

"How are you doing, Mick?" she asked warmly.

"I'm okay," he replied, settling into the chair. "I've been thinking a lot about my future. I feel like I need to keep learning."

Kim leaned forward slightly, her expression thoughtful. "That's good to hear, Mick. What field are you studying again? I can't quite remember."

"Advanced business," Mick said, his tone steady. "I've always thought about becoming a leader. But an associate degree won't cut it. I know I'm just a small guy in a big world, but I like to think big."

A smile played at the corners of Kim's lips. "That's a great mindset. I like that. I'll start putting together the classes, protocols, and costs when I get the time. Things are a bit busy right now, so it might take me a day or two."

"Take your time," Mick replied, nodding.

Kim tapped her pen thoughtfully on the desk. "If all goes well, we can probably get you started next week. Mick, I didn't mention this before, but I'm sorry about your mom. She was a wonderful woman. We had a good connection, and she always wanted the best for you."

Mick's jaw tightened momentarily, but he forced a polite smile. "Thank you, Kim. It hasn't been that long since she passed. I still think about her now and then."

Kim gave him a reassuring nod. "She'd be proud of you, Mick. I'll get the paperwork ready for your future at Dunwood."

Mick shifted slightly. "Do you need me to make a payment now?"

Kim shook her head. "No, your mom already covered your first two years with two separate checks. You're all set for now."

Mick stood, his smile broader but still calculated. "I'm looking forward to this."

"And I'm sure your mom would be proud of the life you're leading," Kim said with a soft smile.

Inside, Mick's thoughts churned. *Damn it, I'm a good actor.* Out loud, he replied simply, "Thank you."

***

As he drove toward Star One Pawn Shop, Mick felt a familiar coldness settle over him. He parked but didn't go inside. Instead, he stared through the glass front, watching Cory Smith lean against the counter, his tattered leather jacket hanging loosely from his shoulders. Mick's mind wandered.

They should be like me. I know what values, morals, guilt, and empathy are. But why carry the weight of those feelings? Why should I show emotions? Let others drown in them; I'll stay afloat.

The thought lingered as Mick drove to McDonald's. He wasn't in the mood to cook. He wasn't in the mood for much these days. A deep restlessness gnawed at him, a hunger he couldn't quite name but knew too well.

Back home, he sat through a couple of horror movies, barely paying attention. His thoughts were elsewhere, on the authorities, the perfect way to stay one step ahead, and the careful planning required to avoid mistakes.

"The biggest opponent I have is myself," Mick murmured to the empty room. *Control is everything. If I lose it, they'll find me. I can't let that happen.*

***

Mick drifted into a fitful sleep, his mind replaying a familiar nightmare. The heavy metal ball in his hands felt real, almost comforting, as he envisioned it swinging. The Devil stood by, watching silently, as always. Time pressed down on Mick, urging him to act before it turned against him.

The doorbell rang, snapping him awake. He rubbed his eyes and shuffled downstairs.

Amy stood on the doorstep, swaying slightly, her cheeks flushed. She stepped inside uninvited, tossing her coat onto the floor.

"Hey, Mick," she slurred.

Mick caught the sharp smell of alcohol and thought, *She's plastered.* "Amy, how are you doing?"

She turned, her expression sad. "I miss your mom so much. My other friends, they're all boring now. They stay home with their families. I'm all alone. My daughter's off at college, miles away. I thought about asking you to go out with me tonight, but that would look bad."

Rejection, in a different form, Mick thought bitterly.

"So I decided to stop by," Amy continued, her voice dropping. "How are you feeling, Mick?"

"I'm okay," Mick replied. "I got my associate degree from Dunwood today."

"That's great," Amy said, stepping closer. Her eyes, glassy with drink, locked onto his. "You deserve a reward."

Control. That's all I need. Control.

But before Mick could react, she was on her knees.

107

22

The Deal

Mick had spent the better part of the week meticulously researching his late mother's jewelry. The rings, necklaces, and earrings were a legacy of a time long gone, their age adding a layer of value that went beyond the glitter of diamonds and gold. His findings left him breathless: over $32,000. The diamonds were real. The gold was pure. Every detail matched the pictures he found on Google. Each comparison brought confirmation, fueling his confidence. He carefully placed the pieces back in his sports bag, their worth almost tangible in the weight of the fabric.

Cory Smith would buy them. Mick was sure of it. He was ready to show Cory exactly how much they were worth, backed by research and determination.

Before heading out, Mick printed several pictures from his search, proof that the jewelry in his bag wasn't just sentimental but valuable. Many of the images mirrored what he held, and he couldn't wait to use them as leverage.

Sliding behind the wheel of his Infiniti, Mick started the engine, his mind rehearsing every move of the negotiation. When he pulled into the parking lot of Star One Pawn Shop, he steeled himself. The place was bustling. Through the glass door, he could see Cory and his staff swamped with customers, while others waited impatiently.

One worker caught Mick's attention immediately. A petite woman with striking long red hair was chatting with a man who had the rugged features of someone with Native American heritage. Mick's thoughts drifted.

"She looks like she's under 30," he mused, the back of his brain flickering with a dangerous heat. The way she kept playing with her hair sent his thoughts spiraling into a realm of desire and disdain. "Control," he told himself, jaw tightening. "Control."

He turned his focus to Cory, who met his gaze briefly, offering a small nod before returning to the customers before him.

The redhead finally approached Mick. "Hi, my name is Brenda. How can I help you, sir?"

Mick's eyes narrowed. His thoughts turned sharp and accusatory. *Is she Cory's girlfriend? A brazen temptress, flaunting herself. Would she dare wear my mother's gems?* His lips curled into a faint smirk. *I'd put them on myself first... and then tear her apart.*

"Uhm... I have to talk to Cory," Mick said, forcing his voice to remain steady. "He knows. He has to finish with those people before he takes care of me."

Brenda tilted her head, recognition dawning. "Oh... you're the guy with the diamonds and rings, right?"

Mick's thoughts roared again, unspoken insults simmering just beneath his calm exterior. "Yes, Cory and I have to talk," he said curtly.

"Okay," Brenda replied, giving a small nod. "I'll get him."

Mick turned to look at the shop's exhibits, his mind racing. *I should be buying some of this stuff.*

Moments later, Cory appeared. "Hello, Mick. How are you doing today?"

"I'm doing okay," Mick replied. He gestured to his bag. "I brought my material... my stones and gold."

"This shouldn't be happening out here. Come into my office," Cory said, leading the way.

Cory's office was a strange blend of personal nostalgia and old-school charm. Trophy animals adorned the walls alongside framed pictures of Elvis, Mickey Mantle, and George Carlin. Mick took it all in as he sat down.

"Nice antiquity... wow, objects of virtu," he remarked.

Cory grinned. "Yeah. I met a couple of those people back in the day. Those were the days."

"Those were the days?" Mick raised an eyebrow, his tone skeptical. "That's from a long time ago... so why are you going out with a thirty-year-old?"

The boldness of his question hung in the air. Cory didn't respond, just stared at Mick, unreadable.

"Let's get to business," Cory said finally. "I have two purchasers who are very interested in your material. I've been doing this for a long time, and I can tell from the look on your face that you're not going to like my offer."

"I agree," Mick said. "Let's get to business. How much are you offering?"

"12,000 dollars," Cory said flatly.

Mick's mind flared. *I should warn this bastard.* He leaned forward, his voice steady. "Double that, and we'll be in business."

"Double it? Are you out of your mind?" Cory shot back. "There are things beyond your control, things I can handle. Sorry, Mick, but do you have any buyers? You don't, but I do. One's in another state, and one's in the Caribbean. You could sell them one at a time, but my guys want the whole collection. The age and uniformity of these diamonds make them unique... 15,000 dollars."

"No," Mick said firmly. "My price is 32k. I've done my research, and that's modest, considering the age of the solitaire."

Cory leaned back, contemplative. "18,000. That's all I can do."

Mick felt the rhythm of negotiation. It was a game, and he was learning to play it. "Why don't I leave the room, come back in 10 minutes, and we start all over again?"

Cory smirked, but Mick didn't let up. "Look," he said. "I know what you're going to get for my merchandise, 22.5k. Let's do it and be done with it."

Cory's expression shifted to something unreadable. Finally, he nodded. "Okay...done."

It took Cory 15 minutes to secure the gems, carefully organizing them in his safe. He felt triumphant, certain he'd struck an excellent deal.

Mick, however, didn't care. His mind wandered back to Brenda. *Oh, that would be sweet. But it would ruin everything...too close to home. Not next door.*

As he left with a hefty check in hand, he glanced back. Cory was heading toward his office while Brenda stood in the distance, her back to him. *Her back*, Mick thought, a cold smirk tugging at his lips as he pushed through the door and steeped into the light.

23

The Impulse That Cannot be Controlled

Summer at Dunwood was usually a time for respite, but for Mick, it was a period of conflict and yearning. Now entering his third year, Mick was still juggling online coursework with summer breaks, a newfound flexibility that allowed him more time to indulge his darker inclinations. A month had passed since his last kill, too soon to act again, by any logical measure. Yet the gnawing void inside him refused to be ignored.

Sitting in his dimly lit room, Mick wrestled with the relentless compulsion that consumed him.

"The push to kill... why?" he pondered, shaking his head as if to silence the question. His lips curled into a smirk, his thoughts darkening. *"Quit asking yourself why you do this. There is much pleasure in it, their deaths fulfill me. Their rejection of me? Fine. My rejection will be the last thing they see in their miserable lives!"*

Deciding to alter his appearance, Mick bought a box of blonde hair dye. Standing in front of his bathroom mirror, he applied the dye meticulously, his dark hair turning a striking blonde as he waited, a towel draped over his shoulders. After washing and drying it, he admired the transformation, a wicked grin stretching across his face.

"Not bad," he muttered to himself.

Downstairs, Mick prepared a simple dinner of spaghetti with meat sauce. As he cooked, the TV droned on in the background, cycling through headlines. There was nothing about the missing girls, no news, no updates.

"Waiting is a good thing," Mick thought as he ate. *"People forget and move on. I should wait months between kills, but I know myself. Fulfillment erodes within days, not weeks. That little mushroom in my brain grows every day, and it's going to explode if I don't take action!"*

After dinner, Mick retreated upstairs to plan. His next target location? Arcane Falls, a memory from his childhood. He recalled a city pool near an older tech school where his family had visited. The pool had no nearby buildings, no witnesses through the windows. Googling it, he discovered it was still operational and hiring part-time lifeguards, mostly college students.

"Friday," Mick decided, writing down notes. He listed potential entry and exit points, employee parking areas, and nearby highways. *"Plan and practice. Aim at the objective. If it looks bad, walk away. But I know I won't, I always act. Those unbalanced cells in my brain demand it."*

His thoughts turned to his tools. The metal ball, his favorite weapon, was perfect, efficient, reliable, and brutal. He dismissed the idea of buying anything new.

The doorbell interrupted his musings. Mick chuckled to himself as he pulled on a shirt. *"Amy,"* he whispered. *"Sad, lonely, and wanting to be fucked."*

When he opened the door, Amy stood there, her expression conflicted.

"Hey, Mick," she said, stepping inside. "I really shouldn't be doing this."

They settled on the couch, the air heavy with unspoken tension.

"Mick, can we just talk... like friends?" Amy asked, her voice soft.

"Of course we can, Amy," Mick replied smoothly.

Amy sighed, her gaze distant. "My daughter... I call her too much, I admit, but she's been ignoring me. She's been going out late at night. At first, I thought she had a boyfriend I might meet, but now... now it's a different guy."

Mick thought darkly, *"The apple doesn't fall far from the tree."*

Amy continued, her voice tinged with melancholy. "My ex is still in Europe, selling to who knows who. Your mom and our friends used to travel, but now they just stay with family." She hesitated. "Can you hold me? I just want to fall asleep in your arms."

Mick obliged, wrapping his arms around her. They sat quietly for a time, but Mick's thoughts began to wander.

His body stirred with arousal, fueled by Amy's presence and the dark thrill he always carried. They sat that way for 15 minutes, feeling lost in each other's arms. Mick was half pumped up just coming down the stairs, knowing who was on the other side of the door. But now...he could feel his erection rising up, hard as stone. His hand slowly and gently cupped her breasts, feeling her erect nipples.

Amy's eyes opened, meeting his. "Okay, Mick... let's do it. But this is the last time. I need to find my dignity again. I need to be a woman, a lady."

Mick's lips curved into a sly smile. "I hear you," he said, and began undressing her.

***

Friday arrived, and Mick packed his sports bag with precision. Black rubber gloves, handcuffs, his trusty metal ball, a blanket, and food for the weekend. This time, he opted for shorts and a tank top, blending into the sunny crowd with his new blonde hair.

As he prepared to leave, his mind buzzed with anticipation. The risk was greater this time, but so was the thrill. The mushroom in his brain had reached its breaking point. Soon, someone would reject him, and he would reject them in return, permanently.

Mick drove down the highway toward Arcane Falls, his mind teetering between his grim thoughts and fragmented memories. As he passed rest stops along the way, he muttered to himself, "Always a possibility," recalling his past. "That time I kidnapped the blonde, so easy. Could it be that easy again? Probably not."

He thought of his father, who had taken him to Arcane Falls many times to visit relatives. "Never really knew the guy," Mick mused, gripping the wheel tighter. "Mom? I knew her better. Good or bad? Good, I guess. She left me with enough to survive, at least."

Arriving in Arcane Falls, Mick navigated to the southwestern side of the city. His destination stood as he remembered, open but not entirely secluded. The nearby tech school loomed to the north, its modern buildings contrasting with the simplicity of the pool area. It was noon. The pool had been open for two hours already.

114

Mick parked in an isolated spot where no other cars were nearby. He noted the hours posted on the pool's gate: 10 a.m. to 7 p.m. His eyes narrowed as he calculated. **Nine hours open. Part-time shifts. Switch-over must be around 2 p.m.**

"Perfect," Mick thought. He reached into his car for binoculars, training them on the lifeguard chairs. A blonde. Two brunettes. The rest of the view was obscured by the pool building. **No guys, only girls.**

As the day unfolded, kids poured in on bikes, parking at the bike rack before sprinting to the pool. Mick's mind raced. **"Too many people. Too much noise. Too many witnesses. Not today. Odds are against me."** Yet he couldn't tear himself away. He shifted in his seat, letting the breeze from the rolled-down windows wash over him as he drifted into a half-sleep state.

By 1:52 p.m., his watch ticked louder in his head. Fifteen minutes later, the shift change began. He watched as two young women, a blonde and a brunette, left together. They laughed softly, oblivious to the car parked nearby. Mick tracked them until their cars pulled out of the lot. Four kids rode up on bikes, distracting him briefly. Then, another lifeguard emerged. This one was alone. A brunette.

His pulse quickened. He scanned his surroundings. **No one but her.** The sound of children splashing was a distant backdrop.

Time felt elastic, stretching unbearably long one moment and snapping back the next. Mick's thoughts fractured. **"What am I doing? Mistakes are calculable. But... I can't stop myself."**

Memories of his mother resurfaced, unbidden. **"She gave me everything. But what did I give back? Nothing but failure." His mind spiraled further. Amy. She was just lust, submissive, and easy to control. Then there's Kim... sweet, kind, and untouchable. Rejection personified. Her face. Her back turned to me. Always out of reach."**

He snapped back to the present, his knuckles white against the steering wheel. The brunette was heading to her car, walking straight toward him. Mick slipped on rubber gloves, scanning the parking lot in all directions. **No one near the entrance. No one on the street. Just her.**

She was two cars away. **"Now,"** Mick thought, exiting his car quietly. He moved fast, calculating every step. As she approached her vehicle, she fished her keys from her purse. That split second of distraction was all Mick needed.

He lunged at her, swift as a predator closing in on its prey. Her scream pierced the air as she tried to unlock her car. She hit the button to open the door, but Mick was faster. A dull thud echoed as the metal ball in his hand struck her head. She crumpled to the ground, stunned.

"No time," Mick muttered. He wrapped his arms around her waist, dragging her limp body to his backseat. Handcuffs snapped into place, and a blanket covered her form. His eyes darted to the bike rack where two kids were locking their bikes. They weren't looking his way.

He slid into the driver's seat, breathing hard but steady. The car rolled out of the lot slowly, blending into the mundane traffic beyond. A wicked smile crept onto his face. **"Another brunette."**

24

Threads of Darkness

The late afternoon sun filtered through the blinds of Detective Andrew Taylor's office, casting a soft golden hue on the cluttered desk. Files, photographs, and half-filled coffee mugs painted a chaotic picture of a mind consumed by unanswered questions. Andrew sat back in his chair, staring at the ceiling as his thoughts swirled.

Months of dead ends had left a heavy weight on his shoulders. The cases of missing women haunted him like phantoms, each one a nagging presence he couldn't shake. He wasn't depressed; melancholy was a more fitting term, but it was the kind of heaviness that sat at the core of a man who knew the odds were stacked against him.

Andrew's voice broke the silence, murmuring to himself, **"No forensics, no leads. Just a ten-year-old who caught a fleeting glimpse of a red car. How do you find a man like this when the evidence is as good as smoke in the wind?"**

He sifted through the reports again, his mind stuck on Melissa, the first woman to vanish. She had known the perpetrator; he was sure of it. There was a connection, something buried in her life that held the key to unraveling the mystery. **"She's the thread,"** Andrew thought grimly. **"But the thread's frayed, and time's the knife cutting through it."**

A knock at the door jarred him from his thoughts.

"Come in," he called out.

Lieutenant Parker stepped inside, his tall frame blocking the sunlight spilling in from the hallway. He carried a thin stack of papers in his hand and a weary expression on his face.

"I've got a list for you," Parker said, setting the papers down on Andrew's desk. **"It's incomplete, but it's a start. These are people within the city**

who knew Melissa. I've been reaching out to her friends, but so far, none of them have mentioned anyone with a red car."

Andrew picked up the list, scanning the names with a frown. **"Twenty-two people,"** he said. **"This can't be it. There should be dozens more. What about the ones who moved away?"**

"Scattered," Parker replied, shaking his head. **"Different colleges, different states. Some don't answer their phones, and others don't care. We're losing traction, Andrew."**

Andrew nodded, understanding the unspoken truth. As time passed, memories faded, and people moved on. The case that once sparked outrage was now little more than a fleeting thought to most. **"Melissa deserves better,"** Andrew muttered.

Parker sighed. **"I hope luck's on your side, Taylor. You'll need it."** With that, he left, the door clicking shut behind him.

Andrew leaned back, gripping the list tightly. **"Luck,"** he thought bitterly. **"Luck won't find her. I will."**

✱✱✱

Across town, the warm hum of suburban life clashed with the macabre reality in Mick's backyard. The faint scent of charred flesh lingered in the air, mingling with the wood smoke that curled lazily from the fire pit. Mick crouched beside the flames, carefully feeding small pieces of muscle and sinew into the embers.

The fire hissed and popped, consuming the remains. Mick wiped his hands on a rag, his face expressionless.

"Not too much at once," he muttered to himself. **"Don't want to make a smell."**

The skeletal fragments had already been shattered and burned; their stark white shards scattered in plastic bags awaiting disposal. He had spent hours in the basement hammering and breaking the bones, ensuring no single piece could tell its story. He liked his methods, efficient, deliberate, and meticulous. But today, he found himself reflecting on his technique.

"I hit her too hard," Mick mused aloud, watching a piece of tissue blacken and curl in the flames. **"Leaves them brain-dead before I can enjoy it. Have to remember that next time."**

Inside the house, the kitchen was a sharp contrast to the grim work outside. The smell of reheated barbecue filled the air as Mick prepared a plate of leftovers from a recent dinner. He hummed softly, a strange contentment settling over him. The last kill had brought him satisfaction, a feeling of accomplishment that swelled his chest with pride.

Mick reveled in his own self-importance, his sense of entitlement feeding his delusions. **"Rules don't apply to me,"** he thought as he stabbed a forkful of meat. **"Just have to act the part. Charming, confident... Keep your eyes guarded. Don't let anyone see what's inside."**

As he ate, his mind wandered to the tasks still left to complete. The bags of shattered bones needed to be scattered across different sanitation sites, and the fire pit had to be thoroughly cleaned. **"No forensics,"** he reminded himself. **"Burned flesh leaves traces if you're careless."**

***

The sudden chime of the doorbell pierced the stillness. Mick froze. His heart began to race.

"What the hell?" he muttered, glancing at his phone. **1:08 PM.** No one ever came to his house unannounced, let alone at this hour. His neighborhood was eerily quiet, the kind of place where even delivery trucks felt out of place.

The doorbell rang again. He stood up, his muscles tensing with unease. Cautiously, he approached the door and peered through the peephole. A man in a brown suit stood on the porch, his expression neutral, but something about his stance radiated authority.

Salesman? Mick thought, his lips curling into a sneer. He spoke through the door; his voice laced with irritation. "I don't want whatever it is you're selling!"

The man outside didn't flinch. Calmly, he responded, "Oh, sorry. I'm Detective Andrew Taylor. Look through your door hole again, I'll show you my badge."

Detective. The word landed like a blow. Mick's throat tightened as he leaned back toward the peephole. This time, the man held up a leather badge holder, its golden insignia gleaming in the sunlight. He lowered it, letting it hang around his neck.

"May I have a word with you, please?"

Mick's stomach churned. His mind raced through a storm of possibilities, each one worse than the last. He wasn't being arrested; if that were the case, the man wouldn't be politely knocking. But why was he here?

Placing his hands on his face, Mick tried to collect himself. Memories of his victims surged forth, haunting screams, pleading eyes, and the image of one lifeless face, her throat a brutal slash, her head nearly severed. He swallowed hard, pushing the memories down.

"Sir... are you there?" the detective's voice called again, this time firmer.

Mick scrambled for a response, his voice forced into calmness. "Just a minute, sir. I need to put a shirt on."

"Okay," the detective replied patiently.

Mick leaned against the wall, his palms damp with sweat. **Why did I even answer in the first place?** he thought bitterly. The kid, the one who'd seen him, was his main concern. He had been so careful. The only loose end was the kid's description: brown hair. He glanced at his reflection in the mirror nearby, his bleached blonde hair his one comfort. **That kid saw me... or thinks he did. But I'll act. Play dumb. No questions answered directly. Lots of 'whys' and 'what happened.'**

He adjusted his composure, cracked his neck, and finally opened the door.

"Hi, I'm Detective Andrew Taylor. And your name is Mick Enderson?"

"Yes, come in," Mick replied, his voice even. He gestured toward the living room. The two men sat down, Mick sinking into the couch, while Andrew chose the chair directly across from him.

The detective spoke with measured politeness. "I'll be as quick as I can. I'm here to ask you questions about Melissa..." He paused deliberately, omitting her last name.

"Yes," Mick said hesitantly. "I remember a girl disappeared a while ago... I think."

"Yes," Andrew replied, his eyes locked on Mick's face. "Two years ago, right before she graduated. Same time as you. We know from friends and acquaintances that you knew her. Do you remember when she disappeared?"

Mick feigned a thoughtful expression. "Ah… yes. She was a cheerleader, wasn't she?"

Andrew nodded. "She was well-known and well-liked. Into sports and many activities in the high school curriculum. I'm sure you know that."

Mick nodded slowly, his mind racing. **Act normal. Say as little as possible.**

"Did any police officers ask you questions about her disappearance?"

"Yes," Mick replied. "They asked a lot of people."

Andrew leaned forward slightly. "We believe she was abducted on the Friday before the week of graduation. I'm sure you've been asked this before, but when was the last time you saw her?"

Mick squinted as though straining to remember. "I can't recall… maybe at the gym when she was practicing cheerleading with other girls. I don't know… Tuesday or Wednesday? I was done with class and saw her in the gym. That was the last time I ever saw her."

Andrew studied him, his gaze sharp. For a moment, the room was silent.

Mick's pulse thundered in his ears as Andrew squinted, tilting his head slightly. **This is the guy,** Andrew thought. **I can feel it. But I have no proof yet.**

Mick fought to keep his breathing steady. **He's bluffing. He has nothing. Just keep control.**

Andrew broke the silence. "Do you know of any friends or acquaintances Melissa might have had an incident with? Something she might have kept secret?"

Mick shrugged. "I didn't know her that well. Everybody wanted to go out with her."

Andrew pressed, "Did you ever ask her out?"

Mick forced a laugh. "Me? Go out with Melissa?" He chuckled again, shaking his head. "I wish."

Andrew sat back, studying him one last time. "This case is two years old," he said firmly. "But we will investigate, probe, and inquire until it's solved. Until the women are found and the offender is behind bars. I have no more questions for you… for now."

Mick stood, walking toward the door. "Yeah… Melissa was a good girl," he said casually as he opened the door. "I hope you can find her."

Andrew stepped outside, glancing back at Mick one last time. He noted the grey Infiniti in the driveway and Mick's blonde hair. **The kid said brown hair. He doesn't match the clues, but… there's something about him.**

"If anything comes up in the future, I may have more questions for you," Andrew said before turning toward his car.

"Have a nice day," Mick called after him, watching him walk away. As Andrew drove off, Mick closed the door, his facade crumbling as he leaned against the wall, the cold reality of the encounter sinking in.

***

The door clicked softly shut behind Detective Andrew Taylor, and Mick leaned against it for a moment, listening to the fading sound of the officer's steps. His pulse hammered in his ears as he thought, *If I had asked about evidence or clues, I would have only made him more suspicious. Damn it... Stay calm, stay distant. Don't overthink. Don't overreact.*

He exhaled sharply and climbed the stairs, peeling off his clothes with mechanical detachment. The bathroom light buzzed faintly as he flipped it on, casting a cold glow over the room. Mick twisted the shower knob, letting the water stream into the tub. He crouched by the faucet, testing the temperature with his hand. Warm. Just right.

But as the water cascaded down, he froze, gripping the edge of the tub. *That kid saw me at Walmart.* His thoughts raced. *How much did he see? Thank God I dyed my hair. But how long until they piece it together? If I move now, it'll only raise suspicion. No, stay hidden. Act normal. Relax.*

The word felt impossible. His jaw clenched, and he let out a guttural scream, "FUCK!" The sound echoed off the tiles, ringing in his ears.

Mick shut off the water abruptly and stalked into his bedroom, dripping. He yanked open his closet, the hangers rattling on the metal rod. Standing there naked, he slipped on a pair of black rubber gloves, their tight snap punctuating the tense silence. From the back of the closet, he retrieved a heavy metal ball, its dull surface cold and unyielding.

He returned to the bathroom, standing before the mirror. His pale, sweat-slicked reflection stared back at him, hollow-eyed. Mick juggled the ball from hand to hand with rhythmic precision, watching himself unblinkingly. Minutes ticked into hours as his thoughts spiraled.

"Mom... Melissa... Amy... Kim. Why do I keep thinking these women rejected me? They're just illusions, symptoms of something deeper, something broken. They aren't the cause of my problem. The real issue is inside my brain." His eyes narrowed as the ball thudded against his gloved palms. *"Those cells are ready to burst, ready to detonate. My need... my hunger to kill, it's like a volcano. I can feel it building, ready to erupt. Over and over and over again."*

The hours dragged on in the suffocating silence of his house. Mick couldn't eat. He paced, restless, until exhaustion finally claimed him at 2 a.m.

***

The dream began as a formless void, dark, oppressive, infinite. Mick stumbled through it, his feet unsure of whether they touched ground or nothingness. Slowly, sounds emerged: the rhythmic lapping of waves, faint and hypnotic. The inky blackness thinned, revealing a shore. The sea was a shadowy expanse, its surface rippling under an unseen moon.

Mick walked along the shore for what felt like miles, the murky horizon stretching endlessly. The cries of seagulls echoed above, distant but persistent, and the air smelled faintly of salt and decay. His path led him to the base of a mountain, where a single torch flickered at the entrance to a cave. Standing beside it was a short man in a bowler hat.

Mick recognized him immediately.

The Devil's hand extended, beckoning him forward. Without a word, the figure turned and disappeared into the cave's yawning darkness. Mick hesitated, glancing over his shoulder at the shore, now shrouded in twilight. The waves seemed to reach hungrily for the land. Shadows danced everywhere, and the seagulls circled ominously.

The cave loomed before him, its mouth a black maw. The torchlight cast long, eerie shadows as Mick stepped inside. The ground was solid beneath his feet, though he couldn't see it. The air grew heavier, hotter, with every step.

Time lost meaning in the suffocating dark. He walked and walked, his breath ragged, until a faint shimmer of light appeared ahead. Turning a corner, he entered a circular chamber illuminated by a ring of torches. The Devil stood at the center, hat in hand, bowing mockingly. The heat was unbearable, suffusing the air with an almost tangible weight.

"Which one do you want?" the Devil whispered, his voice soft but piercingly clear.

Mick turned toward the far side of the chamber, where five women stood in elegant dresses, their backs to him. None of them moved or spoke. "Which one do you desire?" The whisper grew louder, resonating like thunder in Mick's ears. The Devil's tone was taunting, seductive. "You choose. You always choose."

Mick looked back toward the entrance, now swallowed in complete blackness. No escape. No salvation.

When he turned to face the Devil, the figure was inches away, grinning grotesquely. His eyes burned like embers, and his voice boomed, "WHICH ONE DO YOU WANT?"

Mick jolted awake, nearly tumbling from his bed. His chest heaved as he gasped for air, drenched in sweat. The room was silent, the nightmare lingering like a dark cloud over his mind.

25

Can't Take My Eyes Off You

It was a Tuesday morning, and Detective Andrew Taylor's mind replayed yesterday's encounter with Mick Enderson, a man who lived alone in an enviable house with no immediate family left alive. His father had passed years ago, and his mother had succumbed to cancer not long ago. The man was a mystery, cloaked in a veneer of normalcy that Andrew couldn't shake off.

Andrew leaned back in his chair, muttering to himself. "Goes to Dunwood... been there for a couple of years. Parents gone... money in his pocket, nice house. It all seems too clean. Too convenient."

But the facts didn't lie, or rather, there weren't enough facts to tell any meaningful story. Five women had gone missing, and Mick Enderson was the closest thing to a lead. Andrew's gut told him the man was hiding something. But guts didn't win cases, evidence did.

The weight of frustration pressed heavier on him as he re-read the email on his screen:

Detective Taylor,

> I looked at your correspondence for a warrant on one Mick Enderson. His house, vehicle, and any proof of wrongdoing through your evidence simply do not exist. I would have given you a warrant within the hour if I thought it met the criteria for search and seizure, but I saw none. I am aware of your "gut feeling" and your ability as an impressive detective... but there are no proofs to bring up a warrant. If you find more evidence or authentication of wrongdoing, a warrant would be accessible. Keep me informed.
>
> *Judge Emily Kerney*

Andrew gritted his teeth. "Scraps," he thought bitterly. "I'm not eating steak and lobster; I'm sifting through leftovers."

He considered exploring unconventional leads, perhaps reaching out to religious figures in the community. Mick was Catholic, and while unlikely, a priest might have observed something. It was a long shot, but long shots were all he had left.

His phone buzzed, cutting through his thoughts. He swiped to answer.

"Detective Taylor."

"Hi, Andrew. This is Paul Campbell. How are you doing?"

Andrew sighed, already sensing bad news. "I'm fine, Paul. What's up?"

"I've got some bad news for you," Paul began. "A girl named Mary Hall has entered the missing persons list."

Andrew closed his eyes, rubbing his forehead as the words sank in.

"We believe she was abducted Friday afternoon from Arcane Falls, about 120 miles from Ashland. She was a student working at the Arcane Falls city swimming pool as a lifeguard. It's been three days since her disappearance. Her car was still at the pool… no blood, no fingerprints, no signs of struggle. She just vanished."

Andrew sat silently for a moment, the weight of yet another disappearance crushing his chest.

Paul broke the silence. "Listen, Andrew, I know things aren't going as they should. Five missing women now, and not a single lead to track them. The Arcane Falls police will send you all the information they have."

"Thanks, Paul," Andrew said quietly.

"Good luck," Paul replied.

The call ended, leaving Andrew in the oppressive silence of his office.

"Five women," Andrew muttered. "Five missing women, and still no trail to follow."

He clenched his fists, the helplessness gnawing at him.

"Focus," he told himself. "My gut feelings won't put anybody behind bars. Stay sharp, keep moving forward. Before another woman disappears."

Andrew pushed back from his desk, determination flaring within him. Somewhere, Mick Enderson was sitting in that house, and Andrew knew, he just knew, that the man held the answers he needed. But until he could prove it, he was caught in this unrelenting chase, one step behind a ghost.

26

A Moment In Time

The Devil lingered on the shadowy corner of the street, gazing up at Mick Enderson's windows, illuminated by the faint, persistent glow of a late-night lamp. From this vantage, he could see the pale light creeping through the cracks in the blinds, a soft murmur of defiance against the darkness.

"He's not just some pawn," the Devil mused, a smirk curling his lips. "Not some low-cost drifter scraping by. No, Mick Enderson is a singular breed, a one-in-a-million creature who thrives by his own rules. He fancies himself untouchable, above the laws of men." A dark chuckle rumbled deep in his throat. "Ah, but how I'll revel when their handcuffs snap around his wrists."

The Devil's smile faded into a scowl, irritation prickling at his patience. "Still... he's worth my time, I suppose. A moment or two. His work deserves to continue, if only to showcase the filth of this humankind. Let Father see what these slobbering pigs are truly made of." His eyes narrowed, his tone venomous. "Were humans truly cut from the same cloth as Angels and Saints, Father? I think not!"

Upstairs, Mick Enderson stood at his window, peering into the empty night below. A faint unease stirred in his chest, though he quickly dismissed it.

"Shit," he muttered under his breath. "Thought I saw someone."

With a shrug, he pulled the curtains closed and returned to his desk. The glow of his computer screen bathed his face in stark light as he pondered his next move. He tapped the edge of the desk with his fingers, weighing his options.

Should I leave town? Move to another state? Best to wait, it'd look suspicious.

The thought of stopping entirely flashed in his mind, but he pushed it away like an unwelcome intruder. "Stop killing?" he murmured, scoffing at the absurdity. "Impossible." He clenched his fists tightly, the tension burning in his palms. "It's who I am. It's what I do. That...*thing* in my brain won't quit, won't let me. It pushes, whispers, demands action."

He exhaled sharply, forcing himself to release the iron grip of his hands. His knuckles ached as he flexed his fingers, shaking off the stiffness.

"For now, I'll wait," he muttered, as if convincing himself. "The urge will never die, but I can bide my time. That detective... he suspects me. I saw it in his eyes." Mick paced the room, his shadow stretching like a restless specter. "He's got nothing, though. Nothing solid. If he did, I'd already be in jail. But still... he showed up here. Why? He must have something." Mick's jaw tightened as his mind raced. "I'll have to be careful. Keep waiting."

Meanwhile, Detective Andrew Taylor sat at his cluttered desk, rifling through notes on police-priest confidentiality. His brow furrowed as he read, his lips moving silently over the text.

"If the penitent is truly contrite," the document explained, "the priest may guide him toward repentance, encouraging genuine atonement. But if the penitent refuses to amend his ways, the priest may withhold absolution."

Andrew leaned back in his chair, rubbing his temples. "So, it's not as clear-cut as flipping a coin," he muttered. "But it sounds like the priest could hold back valuable information if he chooses to. Depends on the man, I guess."

He frowned, tapping the page with his pen.

"Not that it matters much in Mick Enderson's case. I seriously doubt that man sets foot in a church, let alone confesses to a priest. Still..." Andrew sighed, tossing the papers onto the desk. "I'll talk to a priest anyway. Maybe it'll give me something to work with."

The late-night murmur of the city stretched on, restless and uncertain. In one corner, a detective searched for answers. In another, a killer planned his next move. And just beyond the edges of human sight, the Devil lingered, watching, waiting, and savoring the game.

27

Soul Searching

Nearly a month passed in a blur, and Mick watched the news with a growing sense of detachment. The once-constant commercials of missing women, haunting images of lost faces, and anguished families had begun to fade from the airwaves. As the days stretched on, Mick couldn't help but think that Melissa's parents, having poured so much money into these public pleas and monetary rewards, were starting to see the futility in their efforts. Time, after all, was a silent predator, erasing memories and rendering the past irrelevant.

"Time," Mick thought, "is everyone's enemy." A faint smile twisted his lips. "For me, it's a refuge. A comfort zone. But it's also a relentless foe. The spaces between moments allow people to forget. And that's the thing; time doesn't wait for anyone. It turns its back, just like they all do. Reject you, dismiss you, tell you you're nothing. That Demon inside me doesn't understand patience. It screams for action." His hands clenched at his sides, the thought of his internal struggle pulsing with primal force. "No more waiting. I won't be forgotten. Not this time."

When Mick arrived at Dunwood, he skipped a couple of classes, school had become irrelevant lately, his mind too tangled with other matters, and headed straight for the library. His feet barely brushed the pavement before he saw her. Kim.

"Hi, Mick. How are things going?" she asked, her voice warm and familiar, a soft thread in the chaos of his world.

"Alright, Kim," Mick answered, his tone deliberately neutral, even though the question gnawed at him. "Classes are fine."

Kim gave him a tentative smile, but there was something more in her gaze, concern, maybe, or just the kindness she always seemed to offer without hesitation. "I'm going to head back, but… is everything okay since your mom passed away?" she asked gently. "Things can be so tough at times. My father... he's got cancer, but they caught it early, so he's doing well now."

Mick felt a strange tightness in his chest. *Cancer.* It had taken his mother, and now, it seemed to be circling Kim's family, too. For a fleeting moment, he felt something akin to empathy.

"I'm sorry to hear that, Kim," Mick said, but even as the words left his lips, he thought to himself, *All I have to do is act normal, and I can fool anyone.* The thought was almost comforting. He tried to soften his voice, to make it sound like he cared. "It brings families together, right? It helps them deal with the pain. But for me, it's just... me. I don't have anyone."

Kim looked at him, her gaze full of understanding. "You're strong, Mick," she said quietly. "You'll survive."

For a moment, they just stood there, looking at each other in a silent exchange of something that could've been called kindness, something real, something raw. But in Mick's mind, the wheels were already turning, turning faster than his heart could keep up. *You're too good, Kim. Too pure for someone like me. You're different from the others, but still... I've had a crush on you for far too long. You would be the one to turn away from me. We could never be anything.*

Kim broke the silence, the weight of the moment dissipating with her words. "I was thinking of taking a different class next semester. We've got two different directors here at Dunwood, and I'll email you the list with their courses and class descriptions."

"Thanks," Mick replied, his voice steady, though his mind was far from the conversation. *She doesn't know who I really am.*

"I'll talk to you later, Mick," Kim said, giving him one last look before turning away.

"Later, Kim," Mick whispered under his breath, his eyes lingering on her retreating figure. As she walked, a dark thought crossed his mind, one that his lips would never utter aloud: *Mostly a lady... but sometimes a slut... a whore.*

The words were sharp, cruel, and they tasted bitter on his tongue.

Inside the library, Mick settled into his usual routine. The quiet, the stillness, these were his moments of peace. For hours, he poured over his homework, but more often than not, his attention would wander to the studies that intrigued him. The library, small and quiet, was one of the last places where

Mick could feel human. In these books, he found knowledge, new skills, and a temporary respite from the Demon that never quite silenced its relentless whispers. Here, for a fleeting moment, the rage inside him could rest.

But even here, the darkness never truly left.

By the time Mick arrived home, the sky had darkened into a deep velvet black, the kind of night that seemed to swallow everything whole. His stomach growled with hunger, so he made himself a simple casserole, noodles, a hamburger, and veggies. It wasn't gourmet, but it was comforting. A small, familiar pleasure in a life that often felt far from it.

Then, the doorbell rang.

Mick froze.

Fear wasn't the right word for what he felt; fear was too weak, too fleeting. This was more like a deep-rooted dread, the kind that clung to the edges of your skin, prickling with a thousand thoughts. A long-awaited confrontation, perhaps? Was it that detective again? Could it be him?

Slowly, Mick stood up, his movements deliberate and quiet. He made his way to the door, each step like a drumbeat in his chest. His heart thudded against his ribs as he peered through the peephole.

Amy.

The anxiety that had gripped Mick's chest earlier evaporated in an instant. He opened the door and, with an effortless warmth that almost surprised him, said, "C'mon in, Amy. Nice to see you."

"Hi, Mick," she greeted him softly, stepping across the threshold. The sun was still hanging low in the sky, casting golden beams through the open door, and Mick noticed the distinct lack of alcohol in her breath, a surprise. "Odd," he thought, but the thought drifted away as quickly as it had come.

"How are things going, Mick?" Amy asked, her voice warm as she stepped inside.

"Fine. Could never be better," Mick replied, offering a faint smile. He had expected it to be a detective at the door, not Amy. "Happy to see you," he added, the words flowing more naturally than he had anticipated.

Amy took a seat, her movements graceful, almost contemplative. "I've been doing... some soul searching, Mick," she began, her gaze distant for a moment. "I finally got ahold of my daughter, went to see her at her college. Spent a few days with her. It was good to see her."

Mick nodded, intrigued by the change in her. "Sounds good, Amy. Did you guys... reunite?"

"Yes," she said, her voice softening as memories played behind her eyes. "We went out to lunch. I met some of her friends, some of them are guys. But they're just friends, not boyfriends."

"That sounds like a pretty impressive meeting," Mick said thoughtfully. "Probably something you needed mentally..."

Amy gave him a look that seemed to carry understanding. "Yes, it was," she agreed quietly.

Then she paused, as though weighing her next words carefully. "Mick... the last several times I came out here, it was... well, you know. We need to stop doing that. I was thinking I might never see you again. But... can we just be friends? Just friends?"

Mick's heart skipped a beat at the question. His mind spun with thoughts about his own mother, the endless longing to be friends with her, but never quite getting there. His gaze softened, even though a strange, unsettling thought flickered at the edge of his mind. Could he really do this? Have a friendship with Amy, his mother's friend?

"Of course, Amy. Just pals," Mick said, keeping his tone light, but inside, he couldn't help but feel a curious mixture of emotions.

Amy met his gaze, searching his face for a moment before she spoke again. "As I was saying, I've been soul-searching. Rather than completely ignore you, I thought we could just be... friends."

The words settled between them, and for a long moment, they simply looked at each other, the silence comfortable yet charged with an unspoken understanding. Mick moved to sit beside her on the couch, and after a beat, he smiled.

"I have an idea," he said, his voice suddenly playful. "I just made a casserole. Too much for one guy. Want to join me for supper? Just two pals?"

Amy's eyes lit up, a beautiful smile breaking across her face. She slapped her hand on her knee, laughing. "I'd love to have supper with you, buddy."

Together, they moved into the kitchen, Amy helping him set the table and dish out the pasta. They spent the next couple of hours talking about the usual, mundane things, the weather, their day-to-day lives, without touching wine or any alcohol. It felt like a refreshing change, a small but meaningful step toward something new.

When the meal was over, they cleaned up the kitchen, and Mick felt a strange sense of contentment he hadn't realized he'd been missing. Amy was about to leave, and they stood at the door.

"Well, that went pretty well, don't you think, Mick?" she asked, her voice still warm from the evening's conversation.

"Yes, I must say, it was very enlightening," Mick replied, his words carefully chosen.

Amy smiled, her eyes brighter than they had been earlier. "We should go out to a restaurant sometime, if you think that's okay. I feel... better about myself, you know? Healing. Seeing what's best in life."

"Drive carefully," Mick said as she stepped outside. He stood there for a moment, watching her walk away, the door softly clicking shut behind him.

Once alone, Mick stood motionless, staring at the door for several long moments. "Sex... now just a friend?" he thought, his mind clouded with confusion. The feeling of desire had come so quickly, so unexpectedly, but something deeper gnawed at him, a sense of rejection that he couldn't shake. His mind flickered back to his mother, the endless memories of her pushing him away, and now Amy. Something was stirring within him that was both strange and familiar.

He turned off the lights and went upstairs to his room, trying to focus on homework, but the unsettling feeling lingered. Hours passed as he mindlessly scrolled through his computer, searching for answers that never came. He stood, went to the bathroom, and as the cool light of the bathroom illuminated his face, he found himself staring at his reflection. His eyes were wide open, haunted by thoughts he couldn't fully understand. It felt as if he were looking into the depths of something dark within himself.

And then, from the darkest corner of the room, the voice came, low, but piercing. "How do you feel, Mick?" it whispered, a venomous chuckle trailing the words.

"Confused," Mick whispered back, his voice barely audible, as though speaking too loudly might shatter the fragile tension around him.

"Why?" The voice mocked him, drawing closer. "Your lover wants to be... a pal?"

Mick's pulse quickened. "It reminds me of something..." he replied, his voice distant.

"I know what it reminds you of," the voice said, its laugh twisted and cruel. "All these women rejecting you, laughing at you... turning their backs. You're not getting weak on me, are you, Mick?"

"No... I will be strong," Mick whispered, clenching his fists at his sides. "I will let them know."

"Good, Mick," the voice purred, its words like poison in his ear. "Your work must go on. The message must be clear. Daddy must know."

Mick continued to stare at his reflection, the haunting whispers of the Devil ringing in his ears. He felt the darkness inside him stir, ready to consume him. He turned off all the lights and crawled into bed, thoughts swirling in his head.

"I have to think," he muttered to himself. "Stay away from the officers of the law, but still... I have to find a way to clear myself. There's still... something I must do. Something dark... must think, there has to be a way."

28

Divine Secrets

Detective Andrew Taylor wasn't quite sure where to begin in his search for religious leaders who dealt with confessions, so he did what he always did when he was uncertain: he trusted his instincts and went out in search of answers. His first stop was the largest Catholic Church in town. After speaking with a secretary and another priest, he was directed to Father Gary Brown, who was said to be the best person to speak with on such matters. An appointment was made for Wednesday at 1:00 p.m., and with that, Andrew found himself on the verge of meeting Father Gary in just one hour.

As the time drew closer, Andrew's mind raced with questions, uncertainty, and hesitation. What could he ask a priest? What was permissible within the sanctity of confession? He knew that a priest might hear confessions of violent, even predatory acts, and by religious law, he was not required to take steps toward justice or notify authorities. This knowledge weighed heavily on him as he prepared for the meeting.

He mentally reviewed the facts he had on Mick Enderson. The only witness they had was 10-year-old Rick Reed, who described seeing a man with brown hair at Wal-Mart. Andrew recalled Mick having blonde hair, but he knew that could be easily altered. Rick had also said that the man threw a woman into a red car, but Mick drove a grey Infiniti, again, easily changed. Mick had been a classmate of Melissa, the first missing woman, and though he claimed to know her, he insisted they were just casual acquaintances. But Andrew's gut told him differently. Melissa's disappearance was crucial to the investigation, and Andrew had always considered her case the most important.

The others, four more women, had vanished without a trace. No blood, no fingerprints, no footprints. They simply disappeared. Each one was taken within a few miles of Ashland, and as the distance grew, so did the pattern, creeping outward. Andrew couldn't help but speculate. Perhaps Mick used something like a hammer, or a metal bar, something that could stun without leaving any visible marks. He thought of the possibility of those victims being silently taken, their bodies hidden, their identities erased. But still, no evidence could connect Mick directly to any of the crimes.

If Andrew were in Judge Kerney's position, he knew he wouldn't have granted him a warrant, not with so little evidence. Yet, despite the absence of solid proof, his instincts told him otherwise. He couldn't shake the feeling that Mick was involved. Mick's life at Dunwood, his elusive responses, and the growing list of missing women all seemed to point toward him. Each time a woman disappeared, they had to wait three days for her name to appear on the list, and Mick always had an alibi: "I was probably at home." The timing of the disappearances, the lack of any real evidence, and Mick's consistent presence in each case, all these factors pushed other suspects out of consideration.

But the hard truth of being a homicide detective was this: sometimes, you're wrong. There was no concrete evidence linking Mick to the disappearances. What if Mick really was innocent? Andrew had to think logically, but every gut instinct screamed otherwise. He had to act quickly before another woman went missing. He knew Mick needed to be alone for just a moment, and that would be his mistake.

One woman had been taken from a sports bar, another from a highway rest area. Wal-Mart had been too crowded, too many witnesses. But the public pool in broad daylight, now that was a different story. Mick's options were dwindling, and Andrew hoped that with each passing day, Mick would grow bolder, more confident, and make the one mistake that would bring everything crashing down.

"Should get going," Andrew whispered to himself as he stepped out of his car and walked toward the Catholic Church. He entered through the door on the right and approached the secretary, introducing himself.

"Hi, Detective. Gary will be here in a minute or two. He knows you're coming," she said, offering a friendly smile.

"Thank you," Andrew replied, taking a seat in front of her desk. For a few moments, there was only the soft hum of the church around them. The secretary glanced up at him occasionally, her gaze lingering on the badge hanging around his neck on a small chain.

"Excuse me, sir, are you from homicide?" she asked hesitantly.

"Yes, ma'am," he responded.

"Oh, I was just wondering," she said, her curiosity piqued.

Andrew smiled politely, his mind briefly drifting to the nature of confessions. He remembered the intricacies of the sacrament, how a priest who hears a confession is not bound to inform the authorities of any crimes revealed, under penalty of excommunication. It was a strange, difficult concept to wrap his head around, but Andrew understood its importance, however rare it might be for such confessions to lead to a breakthrough. More often than not, a priest would try to guide the confessor toward repentance, urging them to turn themselves in.

"This is probably a waste of time," Andrew thought to himself. "Mick is young, he'd never admit to anything here. But it could be interesting."

Just then, a thin man appeared at the end of the hallway, walking toward the office. His brown pants and white shirt were complemented by a stole, a scarf-like vestment draped around his neck.

"Hi, Detective Taylor," Gary said warmly, extending his hand for a handshake.

"Hello, can I call you Gary?" Andrew asked, returning the handshake.

"Yes, that's my name," Gary replied with a nod.

"Shall we talk here, or would you like to go out for coffee?" Andrew asked.

"Coffee would be excellent," Gary said.

They walked together to Andrew's car, and as Gary slid into the passenger seat, he glanced around and asked, "Andrew, I'm not really a car guy. What kind of vehicle is this?"

"This is a Ford Mustang," Andrew said with a small smile.

"Has it got... power?" Gary asked, his curiosity evident.

"It's got some muscle and speed, just in case I need it," Andrew explained, his tone light but purposeful.

"My career is a humble one," Gary said, settling into the seat. "I pray before I eat my sandwich and coffee."

Andrew raised an eyebrow and shifted his gaze. "There's nothing wrong with that. I think more people should be that way... it would make for a more peaceful community."

They pulled into Caribou Coffee and went inside. Gary ordered a mixed latte, while Andrew opted for a plain black coffee, no sugar. They found a small table with two chairs, and as they sat down, Andrew hesitated.

"I don't know what to ask you, Gary," he said, staring down at his coffee. "I'm not the only detective dealing with psychotic people, people who live their lives without direction, the kind of people society tends to ignore."

Gary's expression shifted, his professional demeanor settling in. "Andrew, thousands of people live with issues, worries, and complications. Many reach the point where sanity feels like a distant memory. Doctors prescribe medications and remedies to help them live their lives, but they are still children of God."

Andrew shook his head slightly, trying to explain. "Sorry, Gary, I didn't mean to make it sound like I'm looking for someone treating mental disorders. There are people who break the law without drugs or medications... people who take blood... take lives from innocent people."

Gary's gaze sharpened as he understood. "I see. Then you're talking about people who have committed the ultimate sin?"

"Yes," Andrew said, his voice steady but tinged with the weight of what he was saying.

Gary sat in silence for a moment, his thoughts drifting inward as he reflected. "Andrew," he began softly, almost to himself, "when I became a priest, I took a vow. The sins you speak of are real. The sins that people commit can be confessed within our church. This is a substantial and significant part of what I can share with you. I hope you understand it for what it truly is. In Catholic doctrine, the confession is made to Jesus Christ.

The person is asking for forgiveness from Him. The priest is merely the vessel through which the confession is received. The sins confessed are not given to the priest himself; they are being offered to Christ, asking for His mercy. That's how it works; the priest remains silent because the confession is directed to the Savior. I hope you can grasp the depth of that."

"I understand now," Andrew said quietly.

Gary nodded. "I could never give you any information that comes from a confession within the church," he said firmly.

Andrew exhaled slowly, his thoughts heavy. "It's a hard thing to wrap my head around. I've seen so many families suffer from the loss of their loved ones."

Gary's eyes softened, and he spoke gently, "It's difficult, yes, but it's a part of life. When it comes down to it, whose law will you follow? Each state has its own punishments for lawbreakers; some states have executions, some do not. But there are always those who would follow God's law over the state's, and I hope that makes sense to you."

Andrew looked away for a moment, considering Gary's words. "When I became a cop, nothing about this was part of the equation. It's very likely that the people I'm searching for wouldn't ever confess. It's just not in their nature."

Gary sighed, as if he too had wrestled with this truth. "The question we are discussing is real, but by my vow, any information from a confession remains silent outside the church."

Andrew nodded, a deep thought lingering in his mind. "That wasn't a waste of time," he said finally. "I've learned a great deal, Gary. Thank you." "God bless you, Andrew," Gary replied, his voice filled with warmth. "In God's way, you'll find another way to bring the sinner to justice."

They finished their drinks in quiet contemplation and then made their way back to the church.

As they walked back, Gary's thoughts lingered on the conversation. Memories of past confessions flickered through his mind. He remembered one particular woman, Sara, who had come to him troubled about her marriage. Nothing too serious, she had said, but she spoke of a boy, her son, who sometimes asked questions that left her confused. He was usually a good boy, but there were moments when he seemed distant, not quite there, as if lost in a place she couldn't reach. She blamed herself for not spending enough time with him, for not understanding him the way she thought a mother should. It was a confession that stayed with Gary, lingering long after the words were spoken.

29

The Star of the Show

Mick sat at his desk upstairs, absorbed in his computer, his fingers lightly tapping the keys. He flipped open his notebook and turned to the last page. There, he jotted down the hair color for each woman: Mary Hall, brunette, short dark hair. He stared at the list: *Melissa, blonde, Evilyn, brunette, Molly, blonde, Iris, redhead, Mary, brunette.* It was a simple catalog of their hair, their names irrelevant to him, merely labels in the pursuit of something deeper, darker.

As he continued his work, Mick's thoughts wandered to the hole within him, a void that grew with each passing day. "I must fill... the empty hole," he thought, his mind growing darker with each passing moment. "It grows blacker and larger as time goes on... It shudders, but I hold it back... it whispers... but I don't listen."

He hadn't dreamed in weeks, hadn't seen *the Devil.* Mick's thoughts returned to the moment he'd stood over him, the vision still haunting his memory. "I wish I had really cut his head off," he muttered. "It was worse than a nightmare... it's in my memory forever. I saw it... I sliced him wide open... he recovered... and winked at me!"

The memories of his past actions made his body tremble. His mind churned with thoughts of Melissa, thoughts that enraged him as he recalled the lives lost in his wake. Now, all that remained was a black hole, an insatiable need for something to fill it, a hunger that consumed him. It was expanding. It was hollow. It needed *something,* anything, physical to fill it.

He had tried so many ways to distract himself, to fill the space inside him. He went to the gym, but it was never enough. A part-time job crossed his mind, but he felt it was too mundane. He cleaned the entire house, garage, basement, all of it, scrubbing every inch with oils and fabrics, searching for something that could make him feel alive again. To his surprise, he found more treasures his mother had hidden away, gems, precious stones. In her bedroom closet, buried in the darkness, lay a necklace, a piece with two gold chains holding a diamond-filled star. It was old, unique, and expensive.

"Should look into this before I sell it," Mick thought, eyeing the necklace. "It could be big budget."

At Dunwood, Mick found solace in avoiding Kim. He didn't want to see her anymore, though he couldn't stop thinking about her. Her presence was an unsettling void in his already fractured mind. That day in class, he didn't see her. He did his work online and, when finished, headed straight to the library, though lately, his searches were no longer focused on academic subjects. Now, he sought darker material, researching cataclysmic events and forces beyond comprehension. But in his heart, Mick often wondered, *What am I doing?*

After leaving the library early that afternoon, he decided to take the necklace to the pawn shop. The piece resembled a necklace he had found in an old Sicilian catalog from the 1970s, and it could be worth something significant. How did Mom get it? Mick thought. *I don't believe it's fake. Guess we'll find out.*

Star One Pawn was located in the heart of downtown. Mick parked a block away and walked in, bag slung over his shoulder. The shop was busy, and as he made his way to the jewelry display cases, Cory Smith noticed him immediately and nodded. Mick's eyes scanned the glass cabinets, admiring the pieces displayed.

Just then, Brenda, Cory's girlfriend, approached from behind, tapping him lightly on the shoulder. Mick turned to face her, and for a brief moment, he was struck by the uncanny resemblance she shared with Amy, a redhead, twenty years younger, with a beautiful face and an alluring figure. His breath caught in his throat. For a split second, Mick couldn't process what he was seeing. *Could it be Amy? Did she look like this before?* The confusion overwhelmed him, and his mind raced to reconcile the image before him with the woman he thought he had known. But as the moment passed, Mick realized it wasn't Amy, not quite. Yet the resemblance was so strong that for a moment, he had believed it could be her.

It was a brief, disorienting moment, but it left Mick unsettled.

"Hi... your name is...?" Brenda asked, her voice light, with a hint of curiosity.

Mick bristled at the question. He never liked using his name. He replied flatly, "I know Cory, I've dealt with him before."

"Oh, yes, I remember you," Brenda said with a smile, her eyes flicking toward Cory. "You sold lots of diamonds and necklaces to Cory a while ago. He made quite a bit of money off them."

Mick glanced over at Cory, who was shaking his head in amusement. Cory was caught up with another customer, but his eyes were always on Mick, even as he dealt with the crowd.

"Oops, excuse me," Brenda murmured, taking a step back as she moved toward Cory to help manage the customers. After a brief exchange, she returned to Mick, her presence unmistakable.

"Hi, how are you doing?" Cory finally approached Mick with a warm smile.

"Not bad," Mick replied, his voice tinged with indifference. "I was exploring my mom's bedroom again and found some more gems."

"Better than the last ones?" Cory asked, clearly intrigued.

"Better," Mick said, a glint of anticipation in his eyes. "I'll let you photograph it and figure out what it's worth. Your girlfriend mentioned you made a lot of money off the last ones."

Cory shot a pointed look at Brenda from across the room. "She doesn't know how to keep her mouth shut."

Mick caught the subtle tension between them. A knowing smile played at the corners of his lips. He could sense that their relationship wasn't as smooth as it seemed. His attention, however, kept drifting back to Brenda. She was so damn much like Amy. His mind buzzed as his eyes fixed on her, her fiery red hair, the way she moved, the way she carried herself. It was like his memories had suddenly come to life before him.

Cory, unaware of Mick's distraction, grinned as he grabbed his camera. "I'll get my camera and we'll take a look at what we've got." He headed toward his office with a sense of purpose.

Mick watched Brenda again, her posture subtly different than Amy's, but still eerily familiar. Her expression was vacant, and her movements seemed practiced, like she had mastered the art of appeasing her boss in ways that weren't entirely professional. Mick couldn't help but feel a flicker of judgment. She wasn't very bright, he thought, probably hadn't even graduated high school. But she had a way of drawing him in, a magnetic aura that reminded him too much of someone he wished he could forget.

Cory returned with the camera, a white cloth in hand to lay over the glass counter for better lighting. Mick crossed the floor toward him, and Cory set the cloth over the display case, preparing to take photos of the necklace Mick had brought. It was star-shaped, with two delicate gold chains draped from its points. Mick could see Cory's poker face falter for just a moment as he gazed at the piece. Mick knew that look all too well. The necklace was something special.

"Wow," Cory breathed, as he gently laid the necklace on the cloth, his eyes widening with appreciation. He began snapping pictures with intense focus, already thinking of the high-end buyers who might want it.

Mick's gaze lingered on Brenda, his mind racing. Cory was oblivious to the undercurrent of tension in the room, too absorbed in his work. Mick couldn't help but wonder if he had seen this before, this feeling, this attraction to a woman who looked so much like Amy. He wasn't sure if it was the resemblance that drew him in or the yearning for something that seemed out of reach. But every time he looked at Brenda, it was like the past, the unspoken, the painful memories, were clawing at him, demanding attention.

Cory finished taking the last of the photos and looked up. "Well," he said, scrutinizing the necklace, "the quality is real, gold, diamonds... but we'll need to trace its origins to know its true value."

Mick nodded, but his thoughts were elsewhere. "I saw pictures of something similar in the library," he said, his voice flat. "Looks like it was made in Sicily."

"Let's find out first," Cory said with a shrug, glancing back at Mick. "It may not be worth what you think."

Mick smiled inwardly. He had a feeling this necklace was more valuable than Cory realized. "My cards are better than yours," Mick thought, a silent confidence stirring inside him.

He placed the necklace back in his bag and stood up, the momentary distraction of Brenda's presence still lingering in his thoughts.

"Is that the only one?" Cory asked, his voice probing, his eyes flicking toward Mick's bag.

"No... no more," Mick replied, his voice curt. He turned to leave, but not before giving Brenda one last lingering look. She was helping another customer, her curves accentuated by her form-fitting uniform, her movements graceful, but mechanical. Mick's eyes lingered a little too long, his mind working through thoughts he couldn't escape.

As Mick reached his car, he paused. He pulled out his phone and checked the time, 6:15 p.m. He glanced at the pawn shop's hours: 8 p.m. on weekdays.

Not wanting to miss his opportunity, he walked past his car and continued for two blocks, his mind still on Brenda. He ducked into an Italian restaurant, the warm aroma of marinara sauce filling the air.

"Name, please?" the waitress asked as she greeted him at the door.

"Elvis," Mick replied, forcing himself to sound casual.

"Just you?" she asked, her eyebrows arched in polite curiosity.

"Yes, just me," Mick confirmed, settling into the booth she led him to.

After placing his order, Mick ate slowly, glancing at the time every few minutes, his phone in his hand, waiting for the evening to unfold as he had planned. At 7:50, he paid and returned to his car, driving to a spot half a block from Star One Pawn, parking strategically so he could watch for any sign of Brenda leaving.

As the clock struck 8:15, Mick saw her. She stepped out of the pawn shop, heading in the opposite direction of his car. His pulse quickened. He waited a moment, then slowly followed her, keeping his distance. She turned onto a main road, her pace steady. Mick kept a careful eye on her, not too close, not too far.

She eventually turned onto 48th Avenue, then onto Peach Street. Mick slowed as she pulled into a townhouse duplex. He saw her open the garage door with a remote, drive in, and close it behind her.

"235 Peach Street," Mick thought with a satisfied grin, the pieces of his quiet plan falling into place. "Very good."

30

The Vanishing Hour

Andrew Taylor had spoken with the Arcane Falls officers more times than he cared to count. Each conversation left him with the same gnawing frustration. He had toyed with the idea of driving down there himself, but what was the point? There was nothing to investigate.

Mary Hall had vanished without a trace. Her car remained in the parking lot, an eerie monument to her sudden disappearance. No clues, no witnesses, nothing. Just another woman swallowed by the void.

"This guy is lucky... too damn lucky," Andrew thought bitterly, pacing his living room. "Five women missing, and not a single solid lead. It has to be one guy. A gang would've slipped up by now, left a trail of mistakes. But this? This is precise. Calculated." He clenched his fists. "Mary Hall adds nothing to the evidence. No slip-ups, no signs. Going for a warrant now would be a waste of time. All I can do is wait. Wait for him to screw up." The thought made his stomach churn. Waiting felt like losing.

In the basement kitchen of St. Cecilia's Church, Priest Brown and Priest Stewart sat over steaming mugs of coffee, their conversation veering from parish duties to the peculiar events of the day.

"What was the officer like?" David Stewart asked, his brow furrowed. "Did he press you with questions you couldn't answer?"

Gary Brown shook his head. "Not really. He seemed more curious about the sanctity of confession. Why priests can't disclose what we hear. He didn't ask for names or specifics... but I suspect he's looking for someone. A Catholic, maybe. Someone who's done something... unspeakable."

David sighed, leaning back in his chair. "I've never had a confession more scandalous than a husband admitting infidelity. And, of course, I can't tell you who that was," he added with a wry smile. Gary chuckled softly in response.

"Still, you have to wonder," Gary mused, "why would he even bring it up unless he was chasing something big?"

David nodded. "Yes… something about his questions felt… deliberate. He's searching for answers he can't find anywhere else."

Across town, Mick prepared for the night ahead with a grim sense of purpose. The backseat of his car was stripped bare, devoid of food or water. Just the essentials: handcuffs, black rubber gloves, rope, a long coat, and his metal ball. He went over the plan again in his head, every detail etched into his mind.

"She'll drive into her garage," he muttered to himself, gripping the steering wheel tightly. "I'll slip in before the door closes. There's always a button to open it from the inside. Stun her, then finish it."

A cold sweat prickled his forehead. Lately, he'd felt himself unraveling. The thrill that once steadied his nerves was turning into a wispy haze of doubt. But he couldn't stop now. He wouldn't. Each act only fueled his confidence, even as the risks mounted. "The Devil was right," he whispered, recalling the voice in his mind. "Once you start, you never stop. Fulfillment. Fill the void."

Mick drove past Star One Pawn Shop, his eyes scanning the glass walls for his target. There she was, moving behind the counter. "It's Thursday," he noted, glancing at the dashboard clock. "Store closes at eight. Thirty, maybe forty minutes before she heads home. If she goes straight home, I'll be ready. If not…" He trailed off, his jaw tightening. She looked so much like Amy.

By 8:07, Mick had positioned himself outside her townhouse near the pond. Luck seemed to favor him tonight. Both of her garage spaces were empty, as was the unit next door. He parked in the shadows, pulling his coat tighter around him. The probability of being seen gnawed at the edges of his confidence, but he dismissed the thought. He was too far in to turn back now.

Mick circled the block several times, scanning for anything out of place. A couple of cars passed by, but none lingered. Confidence surged through him, his longing for Brenda eclipsing every doubt.

"If someone sees me, if it looks bad, I'll drive away and disappear," Mick thought. Yet, deep down, he knew how perilous this was. His mind whispered warnings, but his obsession drowned them out.

At 8:27, Mick parked beside her garage in her neighbor's lot, scanning his surroundings. The street was eerily quiet. He eased his car door open, careful to keep his movements silent. Minutes ticked by. A car passed, its headlights cutting through the dim street before fading away. Mick's heart pounded, but he stayed rooted.

"Everything about this feels wrong," he thought, sweat beading on his forehead. "Drive away." Yet, his need clawed at him. "Damn it... I have to have her!" It was the first time he felt true fear before an abduction, the awareness of witnesses gnawing at his resolve.

Too late to retreat. Brenda's garage door began to open. Her car was half a block away, its headlights glinting against the dusky sky. Mick froze as her lights swept over his car, willing himself invisible. The vehicle glided into the garage, its beam disappearing as the door began to lower.

The moment demanded precision. Mick slipped out of his car, sprinting to the garage with practiced speed. He ducked under the closing door, careful to avoid the sensor. Black gloves on, the iron ball ready in his hand.

Brenda was halfway out of her car, purse in hand, when she saw him. Recognition flashed across her face. In a heartbeat, he struck. The iron ball connected with a sickening thud, and she crumpled to the cement, dazed and vulnerable.

Mick wasted no time. He hit the garage door button, reversing its descent, and hoisted Brenda over his shoulder. Her purse dropped to the ground, forgotten. The door had barely opened wide enough when he carried her out, securing her in the backseat of his car. Her hands were cuffed, her legs bound with rope, and a blanket thrown over her to muffle any sound. Mick started the car and pulled onto the street, keeping his movements deliberate and calm.

But the silence broke. A faint rustling came from the backseat. His pulse spiked as Brenda stirred. Then, she screamed. "Help me! God, help me!" Her voice pierced the quiet night, raw with terror.

Mick glanced back, only to be met with a fierce kick to his face. Pain exploded across his cheek as he swerved, cursing under his breath. A police car appeared two blocks away, its lights a distant threat as it turned a corner.

Brenda's cries grew frantic. "Why? Why are you doing this? Help me!" Her legs thrashed against her bindings, another kick grazing his jaw. Mick struggled to keep control, one hand on the wheel, the other wrestling her tied legs. He veered into a parking lot, the car jerking to a stop.

"Time is killing me," he thought bitterly. "Should've left her alone. But I had to have her."

He turned, his face contorted with frustration. Brenda's legs lashed out again, this time pinning him against the roof. Her screams echoed in the confined space. Desperation overtook him. With a swift motion, he struck her twice with the iron ball. Her cries faded into silence.

Mick sat back, chest heaving. Blood trickled from cuts on his face, but he ignored the sting. The police car was gone. The street was empty. No witnesses.

When he reached his garage, he parked and left Brenda in the car, her lifeless form draped in shadow. Upstairs, Mick inspected his battered reflection. A gash above his eye, bruises darkening his jaw.

"Stupid," he muttered, dabbing at the blood. "Damn stupid. Should've done it differently." He knew he couldn't risk a clinic. The evidence, the questions. Everything had to heal naturally. As he cleaned himself up, he resolved to disappear for a while. Let the chaos settle.

"Foolish," he whispered, the weight of his actions sinking in. But regret was fleeting. The void still needed to be filled.

31

The Voice in the Dark

Mick lay restless, drifting in and out of sleep, caught between the waking world and the endless abyss of nightmares. The sleep disorder that plagued him was no mere coincidence; it was the result of his own reckless actions, an insidious pattern carved deep into his psyche. The residue of his past deeds lingered in his brain, gnawing at him, making every night a battle for peace. Sleep felt more like a distant memory now, its sweet embrace forever slipping through his fingers. His mind churned, never able to forget, never able to release the weight of his choices. The questions echoed in his thoughts: *Am I seeing objects... or dreaming them?*

Mick felt like he had lost time; it had been a couple of days since Brenda's death, and the scars on his face were easily visible. He longed for a shower, to cleanse not only his body but the filth that had become ingrained in his soul. Yet, Brenda's body still awaited him. "Take a shower when work is done," he muttered to himself, trying to ignore the gnawing dread in his chest. He dressed mechanically, the motions familiar but distant. Breakfast came next: eggs, toast, the simple hum of the news on the TV. Nothing about Brenda. He knew it was too early. There were no words to say, no explanations to offer.

Stepping into the garage, Mick was met with the sight of his red car, still swathed in its protective canvas, and beside it, his Infiniti. A faint, acrid odor hit him as he opened the door of his grey Infiniti. Brenda's lifeless body, stiff, cold, and pungent, greeted him like a grim reminder of his actions. With a grunt, Mick pulled out a large piece of canvas, the remnants of a previous cover for his red car. It barely fit in the tight space. He moved her with an unsettling detachment, dragging her twisted form across the fabric. Her forehead was marred with massive welts, her eyes half-open, staring at nothing.

He felt an odd sense of detachment as he worked, almost as if the fulfillment once felt had begun to slip away. Time had dulled the edges of his satisfaction. What used to last for days now faded in hours, or less. The thrill, the power, it was still there, but weaker, diminishing with every life he took.

Mick struggled to lift her from the car, pulling her awkwardly across the canvas. The rope around her legs remained, but the handcuffs were removed. Her body was contorted in unnatural angles, a grotesque puzzle of limbs and twisted flesh. He placed weights, old tools, anything heavy enough to make her sink, before rolling her over the canvas and binding it with wire. He opened the trunk, her weight too much for him to bear without effort. She wouldn't float. He was done with burning flesh and hammering bones. This method, grim and final, felt almost... efficient.

He drove his grey Infiniti for what seemed like hours, the miles stretching out before him until he reached the Small Tigris River, a place where his father had taken him to fish as a boy. The memory, now tainted with the weight of his crimes, made his stomach churn. The gravel road was empty, no cars, no life. He parked the car, opened the trunk, and pulled her out. She was heavy, massive, her body a sinking anchor in his hands. He carried her to the water's edge, the stillness of the river mocking him. The water was deep here, dark, and unseen. With a final glance at the corpse, Mick threw her in, watching as the splash created a momentary disturbance before the water closed in around her, smooth and slow.

He stood there for a long moment, the weight of it all settling on his chest. "This is your burial ground, Brenda," he whispered to the silent air. "This is not how I wanted it to go." His face burned where the cuts marred his flesh, shallow but painful, each bruise a reminder of the violence that had spiraled out of control. "I thought you looked so much like Amy," he muttered, voice thick with regret, "I thought we'd have fun. But no." His mind twisted with confusion, the chaos of it all seeping into his thoughts. *Was that why I killed you?* His brain was a storm, the voices of his past and present colliding. *Stop asking yourself questions,* he commanded inwardly. *She's dead now. Who cares?*

That night, sleep offered him no reprieve. The hours stretched on, each one more unbearable than the last. His eyes remained wide open in the darkness, his mind a battlefield of unanswered questions. "The day I killed Melissa," he whispered to the silence, "my fulfillment was foiled by that... thing... the Devil, he called himself... was he the Devil?" The memory of that day cut through him like a blade, the vivid image of the deep gash across his neck, the impossible healing that followed. The wound had sliced him open, but it had closed just as quickly. The man had smiled and winked... as the cut disappeared.

"Why... do I do this?" Mick whispered into the void.

"Because," a voice rumbled in response, deep and ominous, barely more than a vibration.

"Because they..." Mick's voice faltered.

"Reject you," the voice replied, cold and unwavering.

"But... why would they reject me?" Mick's words were slow, as though speaking them might make the answer clearer.

"No one cares about your feelings, your loneliness, your guilt or shame," the voice continued, its tone dripping with disdain. "They believe they are better than you. You are nothing but a pawn."

Mick's mind reeled. Was this the Devil? Or his own fractured subconscious? The lines between the two were blurred beyond recognition.

"Amy never felt that way," he said, his voice barely a murmur.

"Amy used you," the voice hissed. "You were her satisfaction. Your relationship was hidden, just as she saw fit. That could be why you killed Brenda."

Mick lay in the dark, his eyes wide open but seeing nothing. The night swallowed him whole, his mind a whirlwind of thoughts he couldn't escape. Finally, the first light of dawn crept through the window, casting a weak glow across the room. But Mick remained lost in the shadows, the echoes of his actions still ringing in his ears.

32

Clues and Contradictions

A few days later, Detective Andrew Taylor was immersed in his usual police duties, maintaining order at the station, when his cell phone buzzed.

"Detective Taylor," he answered.

"Hey Andy, it's Paul Campbell. How's everything going?"

"Ah... it's going," Andrew replied, though the weariness in his voice betrayed him. He had a sinking feeling about what was coming next. "What's new, Paul? Please don't tell me..."

"I'm sorry, Andy," Paul said, his tone heavy with regret. "Her name is Brenda Carter. She's the latest addition to the missing persons list. There's one thing you might find interesting, though. You've been saying the killer is connected to Ashland. Well, we believe Brenda was taken from her home there. Evidence is scarce, but you may be onto something."

Andrew didn't respond immediately, his mind already racing. "Should I put in another search warrant for Mick Enderson?" he wondered. "Probably not. The judge would never approve it without stronger evidence. There's nothing clear pointing to him... yet."

"Andy? You still there?" Paul prompted.

"Yeah, just thinking," Andrew said. "Do you have any details on Brenda?"

"I've got some notes here," Paul replied. "Her mother called in a few days ago. Brenda had missed several days of work, and her mom couldn't reach her. I'll send you a picture. She's 29. Her mom mentioned she worked at Star One Pawn Shop for her boyfriend, Cory Smith, he's the owner. Her car was found at her townhouse. One of our officers checked it out, but everything looked perfectly normal. No signs of a struggle, no blood. She just vanished."

"Thanks, Paul. I'll take it from here," Andrew said, his voice resolute.

After ending the call, he quickly pulled up the address for Star One Pawn Shop and set out. On the way, he contacted the station secretary to find out which officer had checked Brenda's home. Officer Ferguson had handled it.

"Ferguson, did you find anything unusual at Brenda Carter's place?" Andrew asked over the phone.

"No, sir. Everything seemed standard, nothing out of place, no signs of a struggle. Her neighbors didn't notice anything unusual, either. It was as if she just disappeared," Ferguson replied.

"Alright, thanks," Andrew said, hanging up. He mulled over the killer's pattern. "He plans carefully, but he's getting reckless. His first kill was here, then 30 miles away at a sports bar, 80 miles away at a rest stop, 220 miles away at a Walmart, and then 120 miles back at Arcane. Now he's back here. It's one big, cocky circle."

When Andrew arrived downtown at Star One Pawn Shop, he parked and surveyed the area. "If he grabbed her here, her car wouldn't have been left at her home. Did Brenda know her abductor? Let's find out."

Inside the shop, Cory Smith was on the phone but hastily ended the call when Andrew walked in. The shop was quiet, with Cory as the only worker.

"Can I help you, officer?" Cory asked, glancing at the badge hanging around Andrew's neck.

"I have some questions about Brenda Carter," Andrew said. "She worked here, correct? She's been reported missing. Her mother hasn't been able to contact her for days. When did you last see her?"

"The last time I saw her was a couple of days ago. She worked her shift, and when we closed, she left through the front door. That's the last I saw of her," Cory said. His expression was unreadable, but Andrew's sharp gaze lingered on him.

"According to her mother, your relationship wasn't strictly professional. Now she's missing," Andrew said, his tone unwavering.

Cory hesitated, then looked down. "She was a good girl. I'd never harm her," he said quietly.

"I'll need to see your business records, the names of buyers and sellers," Andrew said.

"Alright," Cory said, disappearing into his office. He returned with two thick books. "These are my records for the past year. I use them for taxes."

Andrew took the books and began flipping through them. The silence stretched, making Cory visibly uncomfortable.

"Have you ever seen a man, about six feet tall, early twenties, short dark hair, in good shape, usually alone?" Andrew asked without looking up.

"No, not that I recall," Cory said, though his thoughts betrayed him. "He's probably looking for that guy with the expensive necklaces. No way I'm telling him about that."

Andrew paused, then asked, "Are you sure these are all the records for your business transactions?"

"Yes, sir," Cory snapped. "Jesus, I wish Brenda were here. I need her to work. That's everything!"

Andrew closed the books, his mind racing. Something about Cory didn't sit right with him. But for now, he had to move carefully. There were still too many pieces missing from the puzzle.

33

The Clock is Ticking

Andrew Taylor had a growing file on the mysterious disappearances of women in his region. Each name was a thread in a grim tapestry, but to Andrew, the women often felt more like statistics than individuals. He knew their stories, their patterns, but not their last names. They were victims, shadows in the puzzle he couldn't yet solve.

A seasoned detective with an uncanny knack for intuition, Andrew trusted his gut even when the evidence was thin. His instincts, sharpened by years in the field, told him the disappearances were no coincidence. The first woman, Melissa, vanished late on a Friday afternoon, last seen at her high school. The details pointed to something deliberate. Andrew was convinced she knew her abductor. Not a fact, just a conclusion.

Then there was Evelyn, who disappeared from a sports bar parking lot, 30 miles away. That abduction was meticulously planned. Unlike Melissa's case, this one bore the mark of careful calculation. The pattern grew more chilling with each new disappearance: Molly, taken at a rest stop on a desolate stretch of highway 80 miles from Ashland; Iris, abducted from a Walmart 220 miles away, a crime witnessed only by a young boy who couldn't provide more than a fleeting detail, the abductor drove a red car. But Andrew knew Mick Enderson, one of his suspects, drove a grey Infiniti. How did that fit? Could Mick have seen the boy and changed his plans? Mick swore he hadn't.

Mary was taken from a city pool in Arcane Falls, 120 miles from Ashland. By then, the offender was growing sloppy, his confidence swelling. Brenda, the latest victim, had been abducted from her own home in Ashland. The proximity to the starting point wasn't lost on Andrew. The predator was circling back, taunting the boundaries of safety.

Six women. Six lives stolen. And not a shred of definitive evidence to tie anyone to the crimes. Andrew had worked tirelessly to eliminate suspects, leaving him with only a few possibilities. Mick Enderson remained his prime suspect, but Andrew knew the case against him was far from airtight.

"If I were the judge, I wouldn't give me a warrant to search Mick's place either," Andrew muttered bitterly to himself.

Mick, a loner since his mother's death, fit the profile in unsettling ways. He traveled to locations where the women vanished, lingering and watching, waiting for the perfect moment to strike. The abductions at the Walmart and the city pool didn't align with Mick's usual precision, a sign to Andrew that the predator was becoming emboldened and careless.

"He'll make a mistake," Andrew murmured to himself. "He has to. And when he does, I'll be ready."

Melissa's case still haunted Andrew. She was the first. She hadn't gone home that Friday night. Her parents confirmed she hadn't been in her room the next morning. Somewhere between the school parking lot and the quiet streets of her neighborhood, she had vanished. Unlike the other cases, Melissa had hours during which she could have been taken. She wasn't a victim of chance; she was targeted.

The other abductions happened in minutes, random moments where the women were in the wrong place at the wrong time. The predator acted swiftly, a hunter seizing an opportunity. But Melissa was different.

"She's the key," Andrew thought. "If I can figure out what happened to Melissa, the rest will fall into place."

The detective knew he had to tread carefully. His assumptions weren't enough to convict; the law required evidence, and he had little to go on. Still, he believed the women could be found, alive, if luck was on their side.

"It's personal," Andrew admitted, his voice low with resolve. "This bastard has to be stopped before more women disappear."

The weight of the cases bore down on him. Each face haunted his thoughts, each name a reminder of the lives shattered and the families waiting for answers. Andrew vowed not to let them become just numbers in a file. He would catch the predator. He had to. The clock was ticking, and the next disappearance could happen any day.

34

Face to Face with Evil

Mick felt... off. Not ill, not weary, but a peculiar wrongness coursed through him, a sensation as if he were a stranger inhabiting his own skin. It wasn't new, but today it clung to him like an unseen shadow. The dissonance wasn't physical; no dizziness, no pain. It was deeper, an unfamiliar rift within. He moved through his routine in a haze, his thoughts tangled in a web of irritation and apathy.

He didn't want to go to class but had no choice. Pretending to be the charming, affable Mick everyone knew was exhausting. The mask was slipping, and he was growing tired of pretending. **"Nice guy."** The words felt sour on his tongue now, a bitter echo of the facade he'd perfected over the years.

For weeks, he'd simmered in the aftermath of his last "accomplishment." The surge of dominance had been exhilarating, an intoxicating, fleeting rush. But now, like a drug losing its potency, the satisfaction was fading faster each time. That sense of fulfillment was disappearing, leaving behind only a gnawing void. The edges of his psyche felt jagged, as if the careful duality he'd maintained for years was finally fracturing.

He stood at his desk, flipping through his notebook. The back pages were filled with scrawled words, *Blonde. Brunette. Blonde. Redhead. Brunette. Redhead.* Patterns, lists, reminders. He closed the book sharply and tossed it aside, the sound sharp in the quiet room.

Pulling on his clothes, he tried to shake the strange feeling. The morning was bright and crisp, with sunlight spilling through the window, but the day's beauty did nothing to soothe him. Breakfast was automatic, eggs, toast, orange juice, each bite tasteless. Bag slung over his shoulder, he headed to the garage.

His gaze lingered on the canvas covering the red car. For a long moment, he just stood there, unmoving.

"What is it?" he whispered, his voice lost in the cavernous garage. **"No headache... stomach feels fine... so why do I feel like this?"**

Shaking his head, he climbed into his Infiniti and opened the garage door. **"Stop thinking. Just go."** He pulled onto the road, but the sensation clung to him, a fog clouding his mind.

As Mick drove to Dunwood, his thoughts spiraled further. He couldn't concentrate. Everything felt... detached. Like watching someone else pilot his body. His mind kept circling back to his actions, what he had done, what he would do. A quiet chaos churned inside him.

Pulling into the lot near the library, Mick decided he wasn't going to class. **"I'll do it online,"** he muttered. He was tired of it all, tired of the charade.

And then he saw her.

Kim stood by the library, talking to two other students, her smile soft and radiant under the sunlight. Mick's chest tightened. His jaw clenched as he watched her. **"Her back is to me,"** he whispered bitterly. The sight of her laughing with others was a sharp jab to his ribs.

The passenger seat caught his eye, and a small, metal ball rested there. His lips curled into a faint, crooked smile. **"Why did I bring that?"** he muttered, almost amused.

Kim's conversation wrapped up, and the other students left, disappearing around the corner of the building.

She turned, and for a fleeting moment, their eyes met. Mick's heart raced. He gripped the ball tighter, his mind a storm of conflicting emotions.

Kim's pace slowed as she neared him, her instincts tingling with unease. Mick stood there, his posture stiff, something unreadable in his eyes.

"Hi, Mick," Kim said cautiously, her usual brightness dimmed by the weight in the air.

"Hey," Mick replied, his tone flat. He shifted his weight, keeping the ball hidden behind his back.

Kim's eyes swept over his face, stopping at the jagged scars. Her brow furrowed. "Mick...what happened? Your face...those cuts...did someone hurt you?"

Mick looked away, his jaw tightening. "It's nothing," he muttered.

"Nothing? Mick, there are cuts on you! Please, just tell me what's going on."

His gaze darted around nervously before landing back on her. "Kim, do you ever feel like...like everyone's just waiting for you to mess up? Like, no one actually cares?"

Kim took a step closer, her voice softening. "Mick, I don't know what's going on, but I care. You're scaring me right now, though. Please talk to me."

Mick's grip tightened around the metal ball behind his back. "It doesn't matter," he said flatly. "None of it matters."

"Of course it matters! You matter, Mick," Kim said, her voice trembling. "Whatever's going on, we can fix it. Just let me help you!"

For a moment, Mick's facade cracked. His lips parted as if he might say something, but then he shut his eyes tightly and shook his head. When he opened them again, there was nothing but a cold emptiness in his expression.

"Kim," he said, his voice eerily calm, "look over there. Behind you."

Kim's brows knitted in confusion, but she glanced over her shoulder. "What am I supposed to?"

Before she could finish, the metal ball swung down with brutal force. The sickening sound of impact echoed through the air as Kim collapsed to the ground.

Mick stood frozen, staring down at her motionless body. His hand trembled as he dropped the ball, its clanging roll breaking the silence.

The scene wasn't unnoticed.

Across the lot, Ryan Morales froze as he watched Mick scoop Kim's limp body into his arms and carry her to the car.

"Oh my God," Ryan whispered, panic seizing him. He took a few hesitant steps forward but was too far away to intervene. The grey car roared to life, tires screeching as Mick sped out of Dunwood.

Heart pounding, Ryan pulled out his phone, dialing 911. His voice trembled as he tried to explain what he'd seen, but his eyes stayed fixed on the spot where Kim had been, a haunting silence settling over the scene.

Detective Andrew Taylor had been at his desk for over an hour, settling into what he thought would be another mundane day. The bitter aroma of his black coffee filled the air as he sifted through last week's files. The steady rhythm of typing from nearby desks blended into the background hum of the precinct. Then, his phone buzzed, slicing through the monotony.

"Detective Taylor," he answered, his voice steady but guarded.

"Andrew, this is Lieutenant Ferguson. I'm at Dunwood Tech," the voice on the other end carried an edge of urgency. "We've got a situation. A man abducted one of the administrative assistants. A witness is talking to me now."

The words hit Andrew like a jolt of electricity. His mind spun with a thousand thoughts, each more desperate than the last. Could this lead to the end of his personal nightmare? Could this be the break they'd been chasing for years?

"Lieutenant," Andrew said, gripping the edge of his desk, "get every detail from the witness. Did they identify the suspect?" His heart pounded in anticipation.

"Yes," Ferguson replied. "He doesn't know the last name, but the first is Mick."

Andrew froze. Mick. The name brought a visceral reaction, a tightening in his chest, a sick churning in his stomach. This was it. The string of missing women might finally have a face. Adrenaline surged through him, sharp and unrelenting.

"Ferguson," Andrew barked, his voice sharp as a knife, "get it on paper. Witness testimony. Signed. We can't risk him walking because of a technicality. I'm heading to Mick's house now. If there's any chance he went there, I need to find her. Pray he's there."

Andrew's strides were purposeful as he grabbed his keys and bolted for his car. The address burned into his mind like a brand. The thought of tearing through Mick Enderson's home was almost cathartic, but the hope of finding the missing woman alive kept him laser-focused.

Kim groggily opened her eyes. Her head throbbed with a searing pain, and nausea churned in her stomach. Disoriented, she blinked against the dim light filtering through heavy curtains that smothered the windows. The air in the room was oppressive, stale. As she tried to move, the coarse fibers of the rope bit into her wrists and ankles, pulling her back into reality. She was tied to a kitchen chair.

Memories flooded back in jagged fragments. Mick. The metal ball. The sharp crack against her skull. She winced, fresh tears stinging her eyes.

"Oh my God," Kim whispered, her voice trembling like a fragile thread about to snap. She struggled against the bonds, the rope burning her wrists as each frantic pull only tightened the knots. Tears stung her eyes, and a wave of nausea rolled over her as she realized the futility of her efforts. The room felt suffocating, shadows pressing in like silent spectators to her horror.

A flicker of movement pulled her attention. Mick stood in the corner, his posture unnervingly relaxed. The sunlight painted a jagged streak across his chest, illuminating his naked figure with two black gloves and an iron ball in his left hand, a surreal, almost theatrical menace. Her breath hitched. The black rubber gloves clung to his hands, and in one, the polished metal ball gleamed like a promise of violence.

"Mick…" Her voice broke as she tried to steady it, clutching at the thin veneer of calm that remained. "What are you doing? Why are you doing this?"

He stepped forward, slow and deliberate, his bare feet making soft, calculated thuds against the wooden floor. The sickly sweet smell of something she couldn't place wafted in the air. He tilted his head, the faintest smirk tugging at his lips as if her fear amused him. "Oh, I don't know, Kim," he replied in a low, mocking drawl. "Maybe I just wanted to see what you're really made of."

Kim felt her chest constrict as panic surged anew. Her voice was thin, barely above a whisper. "See what I'm made of?" she repeated, the words tasting foreign in her mouth. She tried to meet his gaze, but his eyes were dark, unreadable, devoid of anything human. "Mick, you don't need to do this to prove anything. Please... let's just talk."

His smile widened, but it was a cruel, humorless thing. "Talk?" he echoed, his voice dripping with mockery. "Talk is for people who still have choices, Kim. And you... well, you're fresh out."

Her eyes darted to the door, a futile gesture she regretted instantly. Mick caught the flicker and laughed, a sound that was sharp and jagged, cutting through her like broken glass. "Oh, you think someone's coming for you?" he sneered, leaning closer. "Scream all you want. No one cares. Not enough to stop me."

Tears streamed down her face as she shook her head, her voice cracking. "That's not true. People care about me."

He leaned in, his face inches from hers, his breath hot and unnervingly calm. "Care about you?" he said, his tone mocking. "They care just enough to stay away when things get messy. Just enough to avoid sticking their necks out for you."

Kim's sobs grew louder, her voice shaking with desperation. "Please, Mick. Whatever this is... whatever you think this will solve, it won't. You're better than this. You don't have to."

"Better than this?" he interrupted, his voice rising with a sudden burst of venom. His hand shot out, gripping her chin with a force that made her wince. "Stop pretending you know me, Kim. You never really did. None of you did."

"I'm not pretending," she pleaded, her voice barely a whisper. "I know you're hurting. But this... this isn't the answer."

He stared at her for a long moment, his expression unreadable. Then, slowly, he released her chin, stepping back with an unsettling calm. The polished metal ball in his hand caught the light, glinting ominously as he raised it.

"No, Kim," he said softly, almost tenderly. "The answer is whatever I decide it is. And right now? The answer is pain."

Kim screamed, thrashing against the bonds with all her might, her voice rising in raw, animalistic terror. "Help me!" she cried, her voice breaking with anguish.

Mick's lips curled into a cold smile. "Scream all you want, Kim. No one's coming. And I wouldn't stop even if they did."

The front door exploded open with a deafening crash. Andrew burst in, his firearm drawn, moving with a predator's precision.

"Mick!" he roared, his voice echoing through the confined space. "Step away from her! Do it now!"

The scene before him was grotesque. Mick was naked, his pelvis grotesquely aroused. The man's face twisted into a bizarre smile as if he were relishing every moment.

"Goddammit, Mick," Andrew growled in disgust, his finger tightening on the trigger. "Get on your knees! NOW!"

Mick turned slowly, his gaze unfocused but unsettlingly calm. He let the ball roll from his fingers and sank to his knees, the grotesque smile never leaving his face.

Andrew advanced, his gun unwavering. He locked eyes with Mick, repulsed by the void staring back at him. "You're done," Andrew muttered, his voice laced with disgust.

Behind him, Kim sobbed uncontrollably, her head bowed, unwilling to witness the aftermath. Sirens wailed in the distance, growing louder with each second.

Mick, still smiling, whispered as he was cuffed, "You'll never understand." Andrew's hand tightened on the pistol's grip, his finger hovering near the trigger. A single thought consumed him: one pull, and it would all end. No court, no lawyers, no judgment, just silence. His heart raced as the possibility lingered in his mind, tantalizing yet sickening. But he didn't pull the trigger.

Instead, he took a step back, his arm lowering with a tremor. Suppressing a shiver, Andrew's stomach turned. The nightmare wasn't over, but at least, for now, one woman's suffering had been stopped.

35

The Reckoning

The tension in the room was palpable, thick enough to cut with a knife. Andrew's grip on his pistol was steady, his eyes locked on Mick as he dragged the chair Kim was tied to away from him. The scene was chaotic, unsettling, a naked man sprawled on the floor, an officer with a gun drawn, and a woman bound to a chair, her eyes shut tight, tears streaming down her face. The medical team from the ambulance hesitated at the doorway, their words trailing off as they took in the surreal tableau. This wasn't the kind of call they were used to.

"We were called out here…" one of them began, but the sentence hung unfinished in the air.

Andrew's voice cut through the silence like a blade. "Untie her and take her to the ambulance. Don't worry about him. Do it now!" His tone left no room for argument. The medics, spotting the badge around Andrew's neck, moved quickly, cutting Kim free and guiding her out of the room. Her sobs echoed faintly as they led her away, leaving Andrew alone with Mick.

The sound of approaching sirens grew louder, but Andrew's focus never wavered. He kept his gun trained on Mick as he grabbed a folded blanket from the couch, opened the windows to let in the cold air, and maintained his position. Mick's unnerving smile never faded, his eyes locked on Andrew's. That smile, smug, almost taunting, was starting to eat at Andrew's resolve. It was infuriating, but he couldn't let it show. Not now.

Finally, Andrew moved behind Mick, his knee pressing into the man's back, his gun now at Mick's head. "Put your hands behind your back… now," Andrew whispered, his voice low and controlled. Mick complied slowly, his movements deliberate, as if he were savoring every second. Andrew holstered his gun, keeping the pressure on Mick as he pulled out his handcuffs.

"Why are you smiling, you sick bastard?" Andrew muttered, his voice tight with anger. "I can only hope this is finally over. That you're done with your barbaric games. No more missing women. No more broken families." He snapped the cuffs into place and draped the blanket over Mick's naked body, a small act of decency in an otherwise indecent moment.

The door burst open, and Lieutenant Ferguson entered, his partner close behind. Ferguson's eyes swept the room, taking in the scene with a practiced calm. "Sir, the affidavit has been signed," he reported.

"Good," Andrew replied, his voice firm. "We need to make this easy for the prosecution."

Mick, surprisingly, broke his silence. "I'd like to have some clothes on," he said, his tone almost casual, as if he were asking for a glass of water.

Andrew blinked, caught off guard. He hadn't expected Mick to speak. Every time he looked at the man, he felt like he was staring into the eyes of someone who was already... gone. "Where's your bedroom?" Andrew asked, his voice clipped.

"Upstairs," Mick replied.

Andrew turned to Ferguson. "Go get him some shorts, a shirt, and shoes. Then take him in for fingerprints and photos. After that, put him in cell B. I'll stay here and search the house. We need to make this airtight for the prosecution."

"Yes, sir," Ferguson said, already moving toward the stairs.

Mick seemed to be coming back to himself, the reality of his situation sinking in. There was no fight left in him now. His twisted sense of control, his dark fulfillment, was slipping away. The fantasies that had driven him, the horrors he'd inflicted, were coming to an end. For the first time, Mick looked... defeated.

The hours dragged on as Andrew and his team combed through the house, every inch of it scrutinized, photographed, and cataloged. They worked methodically, gloved hands carefully handling every object. Andrew's eyes narrowed as he noticed the red car still parked in the garage. He'd assumed Mick had ditched it after the Walmart incident, but here it was, a potential goldmine of evidence.

The handcuffs and the metal ball, tools of Mick's trade, were another matter. Andrew knew smooth metal could be cleaned thoroughly, leaving little trace of blood. "He used that ball to stun them," Andrew thought, his jaw tightening. "If forensics doesn't find blood, it could be a problem."

Every corner of the house was searched, every fiber examined. Andrew wanted nothing left unchecked. This was personal. He wanted to be the one to ensure Mick paid for what he'd done. But as the hours turned into days, the weight of the task began to press on him. "We've got him," Andrew thought, his mind racing. "We know what he did. But we still have to prove it. Maybe I should've pulled the trigger."

"Sir," one of the officers called, descending the stairs with a notebook in hand. "I've searched houses before. Sometimes, criminals keep records, memories of what they've done. This book… it's mostly empty. Except for this." He handed the notebook to Andrew.

Andrew flipped to the last page, his eyes scanning the words. A slow, grim smile spread across his face. "Blonde, Brunette, Blonde, Redhead, Brunette, Redhead," he read aloud. The pattern was unmistakable. "Perfect," Andrew whispered, his voice barely audible.

It was a small victory, but a crucial one. The notebook was a piece of the puzzle, a thread that could unravel Mick's carefully constructed facade. Andrew closed the book, his resolve hardening. This wasn't over yet. Not by a long shot.

36

Defeat of the Devil

Priest Gary Brown sat in the quiet lounge of the community center, the morning sunlight filtering through the blinds as he nursed a steaming cup of coffee. His daily routine had been fulfilled, his early walk completed, his muscles stretched, and now the comforting warmth of his "cup of Joe" in hand. The local newspaper lay before him, a ritual he cherished. Most days, the headlines were mundane: weather reports, current events, maybe a lighthearted column about the town's happenings.

But today was different.

The bold headline on the front page pierced through the monotony: **"Serial Killer Arrested in Ashland."**

Gary's eyes widened. His pulse quickened. Slowly, deliberately, he read every word, once, and then again. The room seemed to shrink as the weight of the story pressed down on him. His thoughts spiraled back to a conversation he'd had not long ago with Detective Taylor.

His fingers gripped the paper tightly. "I only spoke of the sanctity of confession," he reminded himself. "I could never break my vow."

The vow.

The words echoed in his mind, unyielding and absolute:
"I firmly intend, from your confession, that you will sin no more and avoid whatever leads you to sin. Your confession goes only to our Savior, Jesus Christ, who suffered and died for all of us."

Gary's heart raced as he remembered the confession, Sara's trembling voice, her guilt spilling out like a flood. A troubled child, she had said. She never named the boy, but Gary knew her last name. **Enderson.** The connection was painfully clear now: Mick Enderson.

His soul wrestled with the weight of it. The sacred promise he had made could not, would not, be broken. Sara's words were not his to share; they belonged to Christ alone. His resolve solidified like tempered steel. The vow was unshakable.

He lifted the coffee to his lips, taking a slow, deliberate sip, grounding himself in the moment.

And yet, twenty feet away, another presence lingered in the lounge.

The Devil sat quietly, sipping his own coffee, his piercing gaze fixed directly on Priest Brown. A small, almost imperceptible smirk tugged at the corners of his mouth.

There was something about this priest, this quiet, unyielding man of faith, that intrigued him. He admired Gary's purity, his strength, his unshakable commitment to his calling.

"Good men like him truly exist," the Devil mused, his crimson eyes narrowing with something almost akin to respect. He leaned back in his chair, his gaze never wavering.

"I just wish he were on my side."

The Devil took another sip, his presence as chilling as it was silent. But Gary, absorbed in his thoughts and anchored by his faith, never noticed the dark figure watching him.

37

Weight of Redemption

Andrew paced outside the interrogation room, his jaw clenched as he fought to steady his breath. Days of waiting for the forensic results had felt like an eternity. Now, they had enough to tie Mick Enderson to the abductions, but Andrew's frustration boiled beneath the surface. The system demanded lawyers, judges, and due process. But deep down, Andrew wished he'd ended Mick when he had the chance.

"One nightmare ends when one disappears," Andrew thought bitterly. *"But here's a new one: sitting across from this monster, knowing I didn't pull the trigger when I had the chance."*

Lizz, the station secretary, had warned him earlier. "Only one person's been allowed to speak with Mick so far, his lawyer. Don't expect him to talk."

Andrew grimaced. *He won't say a word. That smug bastard probably thinks this is a game. I'll make him regret it.*

Inside the interrogation room, Mick sat alone, handcuffed to the cold metal table. The fluorescent lights buzzed faintly overhead, casting harsh shadows on his face. He was dressed in the unmistakable orange jumpsuit of the condemned, his eyes vacant, his posture slouched.

"So this is what it's come to," Mick thought. He felt the weight of his new reality crushing him. No more library visits. No more lazy mornings in his house. No more freedom to act on the impulses that had defined him. His lawyer's words echoed in his mind: *"Say nothing."* And Mick intended to do just that.

Andrew entered the room, the door slamming shut behind him. He paused for a moment, letting his eyes sweep over Mick.

"Morning, Mick," Andrew said, his voice cold but steady. "That color suits you."

Mick didn't respond. He barely blinked, his face an emotionless mask. No defiance, no fear, no remorse. He stared at Andrew with a hollow gaze, his spirit seemingly as lifeless as the victims Andrew knew he'd taken.

Andrew pulled out the chair opposite Mick and sat down. He leaned forward, his elbows on the table, his eyes locked on Mick's. "I've got questions for you, Mick. I really hope you'll answer them."

The silence in the room was suffocating. Andrew waited, but Mick's expression didn't change. He was still, dormant, like a predator waiting for the right moment to strike, or a man who'd given up entirely.

"Do you remember Melissa Miller?" Andrew asked, his tone sharp. "Your first victim. Come on, Mick. Tell me something."

Mick remained motionless, his lips pressed together in a tight line. Slowly, almost imperceptibly, he shook his head. Andrew's frustration flared. He stood abruptly, circling the table until he loomed over Mick. "Evilyn," Andrew said, his voice rising. "Taken from a sports bar parking lot. She was supposed to be married, Mick. Married. And Molly? You grabbed her from a rest stop off the highway, 80 miles from here!"

Andrew's voice grew louder, his anger spilling over. "Iris. You snatched her from a Walmart parking lot in another city. She had a two-year-old daughter, Mick! A daughter who's now growing up without her mother because of *you!*"

Andrew leaned closer, his face inches from Mick's. "And Mary. She was a student. She had her whole life ahead of her, until you ripped it away."

Mick still didn't flinch. His expression remained empty, as if Andrew's words couldn't penetrate whatever twisted world he inhabited.

But Andrew wasn't done. He raised his hand, his voice a roar now. "And then there's Brenda." He pointed to the scars etched across Mick's face. "She fought back, didn't she? I see it. She left her mark on you. But it wasn't enough. Not nearly enough."

With a sudden burst of rage, Andrew slapped Mick across the face, the sound reverberating through the room. "No," Andrew spat. "They didn't do what I would've done to you. They didn't finish the job."

Andrew stepped back, his chest heaving, his fists clenched. Mick sat there, unmoving, his expression unchanged. The silence that followed was deafening.

Andrew stared at him, his fury replaced by a hollow sense of defeat. *You're not getting away this time, Mick. But God help me, I wish I could make you pay my way.*

38

Truth in the Ruins

Andrew paced the dimly lit precinct hall, his irritation boiling beneath the surface. Forensics had uncovered frustratingly little, barely any corroborative evidence to pin Mick Enderson to the missing women. A smear of Mick's blood on the roof of his Infiniti, a faint trace on the car's ceiling. "How the hell did *that* happen?" Andrew muttered under his breath. He could only imagine the scene: a struggle in the backseat, the women handcuffed, one of them lashing out, striking Mick's face in desperation. The metal ball he used to subdue them was brutal, designed to inflict just enough damage without leaving substantial evidence. Still, the fluids recovered barely scratched the surface. Only Kim's DNA had been confirmed, and even that left more questions than answers.

Andrew leaned against the wall, his thoughts a torrent of frustration. *"Assault and kidnapping,"* he whispered, clenching his fists. *"With Kim's testimony, I can push for attempted murder. But it's not enough. I want more. I want him buried."*

***

Downtown, in the sterile courtroom of Askland, a heated battle raged over Mick's damning notebook.

Prosecutor Davidson stepped forward, his voice sharp and commanding. "Your honor, the evidence is clear.

The victims' hair colors were documented in Mick Enderson's notebook, listed in the exact sequence of their disappearances. Blonde, brunette, redhead, Melissa, Evelyn, Molly, Iris, Mary, Brenda. It's not a coincidence; it's a pattern. If Mick had succeeded in killing Kim, her color, redhead, would have been next. This notebook is his ledger of crimes." He gestured to the array of victim photos spread before the judge, their faces frozen in time.

Defense attorney Anderson rose with mock indignation. "Your honor, these words could mean anything. Who's to say Mick even wrote them? The prosecution is grasping at straws, hungry for a conviction. For all we know, the investigators could have planted this evidence themselves!"

Davidson's face darkened with fury. "Are you seriously accusing the forensic team of fabrication? This is absurd!" he snapped, his voice reverberating through the courtroom.

The judge's gavel slammed down, silencing the uproar. "Enough! Anderson, you're better than this. I won't have baseless accusations slandering the hard work of our forensic experts. Do your job with integrity, or I'll hold you in contempt."

Anderson lowered his head. "Yes, your honor."

The judge leaned back in his chair, steepling his fingers. "I'll review the evidence. The pattern in Mick's notebook aligns too perfectly with the timeline of the abductions to be ignored. You'll have my ruling tomorrow."

***

Inside his 9-by-12 cell, Mick sat on the edge of the thin cot, staring blankly at the wall. The room was suffocating, its solid walls pressing inward like the ribs of a whale, threatening to crush him. The dim light from the window slit cast eerie shadows, twisting into grotesque shapes.

"No more... fulfillment," a voice hissed from the darkness. It was soft, serpentine, slithering through his mind. Was it the Devil? Or himself?

"No more... plans within plans," it whispered again.

Mick's gaze remained fixed on the wall, the shadows morphing into sinister animals in his imagination.

"You miss Amy, don't you?" The voice was softer now, insidious. "Her curves, her desires, her submission... That residue still clings to you, doesn't it?"

A shiver ran down Mick's spine. The voice was not external; it was buried deep within him, gnawing at his psyche.

"So young," it purred, "so betrayed by your own mind. I dreamed with you, Mick, a list of glorious hair colors, twenty, thirty, forty. All cataloged, all yours. And yet, here we are. You were caught too soon. You failed me."

Mick's hands trembled as he tried to focus, tried to silence the torrent of venomous thoughts. But he couldn't.

"My mind used to be so clear," Mick whispered, his voice barely audible. "Now, there's nothing but questions. I can't even think straight. It's like... my brain is shutting down."

"Yes, Mick," the voice cooed. "Your body remains intact, but your mind... it's unraveling. You can't focus, can't escape. Reality feels distant, doesn't it? You're losing control. Everything is in disorder now. Everything is decay."

Mick's head sank into his hands. "Yes," he whispered again, the weight of his words crushing him further into the abyss.

39

Fractured Light

The courtroom buzzed with an electric tension as the final pieces of the trial were set in motion. Every detective, lawyer, forensic expert, and jury member had played their part. The Judge, in a landmark decision, allowed the hair color samples to be admitted as evidence, the sequence of fibers perfectly aligned with the timeline of the women's disappearances, a damning blow to the defense.

Mick Enderson sat at the defense table, dressed in a crisp, tailored suit, a desperate attempt to project an air of control he no longer possessed. His two lawyers had spent hours preparing him, probing into his past, searching for a crack in his stoic demeanor. Had he been abused as a child? Suffered beatings? What about his relationships with his parents, friends, or lovers? The questions came rapid-fire: *Where were you when the women disappeared? Did you kidnap them? Where are they now?* But Mick offered nothing, no confession, no denial. His silence was a fortress.

Anderson, the lead defense attorney, clung to a threadbare strategy: an insanity plea. But Mick's indifference unnerved him. Would Mick's apathy come off as madness or malice? Anderson toyed with the idea of putting him on the stand, knowing it was a gamble. If Mick unraveled in front of the jury, his fate could swing either way, insanity or damnation.

The courtroom doors creaked open with a deliberate weight, and the bailiff stepped forward, slamming the door shut behind him. "All rise! The Seventeenth Judicial Court is now in session... Judge Collins presiding!" The room rose as one, a wave of tension crashing against the walls.

In the back row, a short man with a sharp suit and a bowler hat stood, his lips curling into a sly smile. *"I wouldn't miss this for all the whiskey in Scotland,"* thought the Devil, watching the spectacle unfold with morbid delight.

Judge Collins ascended to his seat, his robes billowing like storm clouds. The court reporter positioned herself at the stenograph, fingers poised.

"Mick Enderson," the judge's voice boomed, "you are accused by the state of assault, kidnapping, and attempted murder. How do you plead?"

Mick rose slowly, his body rigid, his face vacant. The question hung in the air, unanswered. He stood there, lost, his perception dulled, truncated by the weight of reality. No smirk, no defense, not even a flicker of recognition. The judge frowned, perplexed by the eerie silence. Seconds stretched into an eternity.

Inside Mick's mind, chaos reigned. **His cells, once obedient, now thrashed like prisoners in revolt, their vibrations collapsing into discord. A fracas erupted within, a symphony of dysfunction. His thoughts, his very essence, twisted and fractured. Insanity clawed at him like a rabid animal.**

"Mick pleads..." Anderson interjected, his voice steady but strained, "not guilty, by reason of insanity." He felt a cold sweat prickling his neck. *"God help us."*

Across the courtroom, Detective Andrew Taylor sat in the gallery, arms crossed. He stared at Mick with a hardened gaze, his thoughts cutting like glass. *"Glad I didn't pull the trigger when I had the chance. He's not all here anymore. This jury won't let him slip through the cracks of justice."*

"Be seated," Judge Collins ordered, and the courtroom obeyed. The gallery was packed with press, reporters, and spectators. All eyes were on Mick, the accused monster. Among them, Kim's boyfriend sat, his jaw clenched, his glare fixed on Mick like a dagger. He didn't want justice; he wanted revenge. *"Just one room, no doors, and brass knuckles,"* he thought darkly.

The trial began at nine sharp. The prosecution wasted no time. Witnesses took the stand, hands placed solemnly on the Bible as the bailiff guided them through the formalities. Lawyers questioned and cross-examined, the dialogue bouncing back and forth like gunfire. Mick watched it all unfold, but the courtroom felt warped, as though he were seeing it through a thick, unrelenting fog. The voices were distant, their words muffled. Reality itself seemed intolerable.

Then Kim took the stand.

The room held its breath as she spoke. Mick could barely hear the questions, but he saw her clearly, too clearly. Her presence stirred something deep within him, though his expression remained vacant. *"My crush on her means nothing now,"* he thought bitterly. She glanced at him once, briefly, before pointing him out as her abductor.

"That's him," she said, her voice steady. "In the suit."

Her words cut through the haze like a blade. She didn't look at him again as she left the stand, passing him without so much as a glance. For Mick, the moment was surreal, the final nail in a coffin of his own making.

***

Mick's mind churned in agony, the weight of the trial pressing down on him like a vise, suffocating his every thought. His anxiety twisted into something far darker, panic clawed at his insides, his nerves sparking with electricity. He felt himself slip further and further away from reality, a distorted echo of who he once was. *His brain cells screamed in pressure, disconnected from their function, drowning in a sea of confusion.*

The courtroom was a blur, but there was one voice that cut through the noise: Andrew Taylor. He was standing at the bench, speaking the words that would haunt Mick's every thought. "That's him. In the suit," Taylor said, his finger stabbing toward Mick.

Mick's thoughts screamed, *"They're like leeches... hungry wolves... smelling blood."* He could feel their eyes on him, devouring him, circling closer, inching toward his soul. The minutes dragged on, stretching endlessly, the weight of time unbearable. *Was this eternity?* It felt as though he had been sitting there for lifetimes, suffocated by the unbearable gaze of everyone around him.

A sudden thought broke through the haze, a fleeting moment of relief. *"Oh God, it's that little boy,"* Mick thought as Rick Reed took the stand. The boy said nothing, pointed nowhere, and for the briefest instant, Mick's heart steadied.

But the trial pressed on, relentless. The prosecutor moved toward the jury, a white sheet draped over a stand. With deliberate precision, he yanked it away. The images were graphic, pictures of Mick's victims. Beautiful faces, frozen in smiles, now forever immortalized in death. They seemed so innocent, so full of life, until they weren't.

The prosecutor methodically laid out the sequence of Mick's crimes, his journals a chilling testament to his sinister pattern. The jury's eyes locked on Mick, their gazes thick with sorrow, disgust, and pity. Anderson watched, dread creeping up his spine as Mick remained an island of silence. *"This is not going well,"* he thought, helplessly.

A brief respite came in the form of a fifteen-minute break. Mick didn't move. His body was a statue, his mind trapped in a labyrinth of thought and dread. His gaze never left the floor, and the Devil, always present, always watching, stood nearby, delighting in Mick's unraveling. *"Poor little Mick,"* the Devil mused, *"You were doing so well. Assassination after assassination, leaving destruction in your wake... but now? You're losing it. You're slipping away from me."*

When the trial resumed, Anderson couldn't help but feel a creeping sense of defeat. He watched the prosecutors, the witnesses, each piece falling into place, each word twisting the knife deeper into Mick's already broken soul. Mick saw his lawyer, but everything felt so distant, so detached. *"Is he defending me... or is he just playing the part?"* Mick wondered, lost in his own spiraling mind. Anderson's frustration mounted as Mick refused to answer his questions, stonewalling him at every turn. *"You're making this so much harder, Mick,"* Anderson thought bitterly. *"So much harder..."*

The prosecution's witnesses paraded through the courtroom, their words digging into the fabric of Mick's guilt. Each testimony was another shard of glass in his collapsing world. His head throbbed with the pressure of so many voices, so many accusations. *"I'm surrounded by enemies,"* Mick thought, his mind reeling. Anderson, ever the professional, did what he could, but Mick's indifference left him with no leverage, no way to fight back.

Finally, the words Mick had been dreading arrived: "The prosecution rests."

The courtroom fell silent, as if the air itself had been sucked out of the room. Judge Collins' voice broke through the stillness, "It's time for lunch. We'll reconvene at 1 PM."

Anderson sat back, defeated. He had been in this position before. He knew the truth: Mick was guilty, no matter how much doubt he could muster for the missing women. There was no escape from Kim's near-murder, no defending that. The photographs of the girls, the chilling precision of Mick's writings, they painted a damning portrait for the jury. *"This is it,"* Anderson thought grimly. *"The only card I can play is insanity."*

He leaned toward Mick, his voice low and heavy. "Mick," he whispered, "I've asked you questions with no answers... I've told you about the death penalty, about the executions. They don't have proof you killed anyone, except for Kim. But your writings, the way you've documented everything, *that* is proof. The jury will see that.

You're guilty in their eyes. They'll convict you, and you'll die for it unless... unless you take the stand. Should I do that? Should I put you on the stand?"

Mick was trapped in a fog, a haze of confusion and dread, his mind barely tethered to the reality around him. He knew he was at trial; he felt the weight of it pressing down on him like a thousand-ton anchor. But beyond that, nothing made sense. The trial, the accusations, the faces in the room... it was all a blur, as if he was watching it unfold from a distant vantage point. What he couldn't comprehend, however, was the chilling truth: he could be executed for his crimes. The thought barely pierced the murkiness of his mind, and worse, he had no idea that everyone around him saw him as something... unstable.

"Um... yes, put me on the bench," Mick muttered, his voice hollow and detached, as though the words weren't even his own.

Anderson stood there, his gaze locked onto Mick, a storm of confusion and concern swirling inside him. *What is he thinking?* Anderson couldn't tell. Was Mick even thinking at all? His mind seemed a labyrinth of fragmented thoughts, lost in a maze of disarray. He leaned in close, his voice barely above a whisper. "Alright, I'll put you on the stand. Remember what I told you, no matter what they ask, you don't know these women. You can't remember them. Got it? Not guilty by reason of insanity. That's your defense." Anderson paused, then added with a sigh, "You should eat something. You look like you could use it."

Mick's hollow response came swiftly, his words as empty as his eyes. "No, not hungry at all. I'll just sit here."

Anderson nodded, unsure of what to make of Mick's apparent detachment. "Okay. I'll be back in 20 to 25 minutes," he said, his voice thick with concern as he turned to leave.

The next half hour dragged on, each passing minute an eternity. Reporters shuffled in and out of the courtroom, journalists scribbled furiously in their notebooks, and the rustling of papers and low murmur of conversations echoed through the space. Two guards kept their watchful eyes on Mick, following the judge's orders with cold precision.

Mick closed his eyes, his body slumped in the chair as exhaustion crept over him. His mind was a battlefield, fragments of memories slipping through his fingers like sand. The last week had been hell, each moment a jumbled mess of confusion, self-doubt, and fear. *What should I do? What should I say?* His thoughts were hazy, disconnected, spiraling inward. *When this is all over, I'll be locked away forever... A cell... No one will care. Not when mom died, and not when I die in here either.* His brain tried to show him some flicker of emotion, but it was like trying to light a match in the rain. There was nothing there. *I feel... nothing.*

The minutes crawled by with excruciating slowness until the bailiff opened the door by the bench once more. "Judge Collins," the voice rang out. The courtroom fell silent, the tension in the air thick enough to cut with a knife.

"Let us continue," Judge Collins' voice broke the silence, his hand sweeping toward Anderson. "It is the defense's turn."

Anderson stood tall, but his gaze flicked to Mick, his weary client, lost in his own world. *Remember what I said,* Anderson thought as he whispered across the aisle, his voice a low murmur, "When the prosecutor asks about the missing women, you don't know them. You don't remember them, got it?"

Mick's eyes remained closed, his mind adrift in a sea of disconnection. He wasn't sure what to think. The prosecutor had aggressively connected him to the disappearances of six women. But Mick couldn't feel anything about it, not a shred of emotion or remorse. He opened his eyes, his gaze drawn to the pictures of the missing women, each smile frozen in time. But one face caught his eye, *Melissa,* and the memory came flooding back, unbidden and unwanted.

A sickening thought slid through his mind, a sharp edge cutting through the haze. *Is that why I'm here? Is that thing the real reason for all of this?* His mind spiraled as the memory flashed, his knife carving into the neck of that... thing. *How could this happen? How could I let it happen?* The Devil, grinning like a Cheshire cat, applauded from the shadows. *I'll never forget,* Mick vowed in his mind. *I'll never forget that wink.*

Mick's mental unraveling had been slow, gradual stages of madness creeping up on him, unnoticed by those around him, but unmistakable to the ones who truly saw. His anxiety, once a whisper, had grown louder, more ferocious with each passing day. His brain had been on fire, seething with rage that hadn't yet burnt out. The people in his life had seen it before he ever did, the madness growing, feeding off his own confusion, until it had consumed him entirely.

Anderson's voice cut through the chaos, pulling Mick back into the present. "I would like to call Mick Enderson to the bench."

Mick's head lifted, his eyes barely focusing on the room. Every pair of eyes in the courtroom was locked on him, journalists, the jury, the entire gallery, and it was like being naked in front of the world. The silence was deafening. You could hear a pin drop as Mick slowly, robotically, stood and walked toward the stand.

The bailiff's voice rang out, harsh and mechanical. "Left hand on the Bible, raise your right hand." Mick complied, his body moving on autopilot. "Do you swear to tell the truth, the whole truth, and nothing but the truth?"

"I do," Mick's voice was almost a whisper as he answered, his words heavy with a weight only he could understand. He sank back into the chair, his posture stiff, every muscle in his body taut as if bracing for something. A chilling silence descended upon the courtroom, an oppressive, suffocating stillness that stretched the seconds into what felt like an eternity. Every eye in the room was locked on him, every breath held, as if the world itself had frozen in place.

Anderson, with his head bowed, moved toward the bench slowly, deliberately. His fingers stroked his chin, deep in thought, or perhaps searching for the right words, his every movement betraying a mind that couldn't quite grasp the gravity of what was unfolding. The air in the courtroom seemed to stand still, as though time itself had been suspended.

186

Finally, Anderson broke the silence, his voice cutting through the tension like a blade. "Mick, I'd like to look into your past. Your father passed away when you were young... and just recently, your mother died. Could you tell the jury about your relationship with her?"

Mick's body barely shifted, his hands flat on the desk before him, his face a mask of detached curiosity, a look so foreign on him it seemed almost unnatural. But then, like a thunderclap from the heavens, his expression shifted. A sudden, violent surge of emotion ripped through him, a storm triggered by the mounting pressure of his circumstances. His body trembled, his mind clouded by the undercurrent of his mental unraveling. The anger that had been simmering, coiling like a serpent within him, was suddenly unleashed.

His cells, already brimming with rage, now exploded in violent fury. He could feel it, his heart pounding in his chest, his blood boiling as the wolf inside him reared its head. The predator in him was awakened, no longer tethered by reason or remorse. The familiar, gnawing emptiness had driven him to this point, and now, there would be no turning back.

Without warning, Mick pulled his arms back, slumping into the chair as if he had been struck by a physical blow. His back pressed against the backrest, the words coming out of him like a venomous hiss. "My mother," Mick began, his voice growing colder, more venomous with every word, "I didn't give a rat's ass when she died."

The words echoed in the courtroom, and the room was instantly filled with gasps of disbelief. Journalists exchanged shocked glances, some whispering to each other, their pens poised, eager to capture the chaos unfolding before them. The prosecutors, their eyes gleaming with the thrill of victory, exchanged sly smiles; they could already taste the triumph of their victory, a moment to add to their growing list of accomplishments.

Anderson, trying to maintain control, stammered, "Well... I think we, "

Mick's voice cut through the air like a jagged knife. "Why don't you ask the real question?"

Anderson, caught off guard, stuttered, trying to play along. "What question?"

Mick's eyes flicked toward him, the intensity in his gaze unmistakable. "Why I killed all those women?"

A collective gasp rippled through the room. The courtroom erupted into a cacophony of voices, whispers, and shouts, the sound of disbelief ringing in the air. Some screamed in horror, others muttered to one another in stunned amazement. "Oh my God," someone cried out, their voice high-pitched with shock.

Judge Collins' gavel slammed down with a force that cracked through the chaos like a whip. "Quiet! Quiet now!" His voice boomed, commanding the room into submission. Collins had seen many strange things during his years on the bench, but never anything like this. This man, accused of killing six women, women whose bodies were never found, had just confessed in the most casual manner imaginable. Collins' mind raced. *If he gives a full confession... this trial would be over so quickly...* His eyes flicked toward Mick, and he realized that no matter how this unfolded, the law could not ignore what had just been spoken aloud. *"Let the man speak."*

The room fell deathly silent once more, as if the very air itself was holding its breath. Mick and the judge locked eyes, an unspoken understanding passing between them. "You may continue," the judge said, his voice now softer, resigned to the inevitable.

Mick stood up, his body trembling with a mixture of rage and some twisted form of satisfaction. His voice rang out, raw and unrestrained. "All these women would have rejected me!" He shouted, his words laced with the venom of years of abandonment and isolation. "They're so nice at first... But ultimately, they reject me! And so, as time went on, I rejected them. I needed to keep my soul... fulfilled!" His eyes flickered with a sickening sense of triumph, as if he were savoring the very act of spilling his truth, no matter how horrific. "Don't even ask where they are right now," he continued, his voice dark and cold. "I burned their flesh in my backyard pit. In my basement, I covered the floor with plastic... hammered their bones to pieces and put them in bags, then delivered them to the public dumpsters."

The words hung in the air like a noxious cloud, choking the room with their weight. No one moved. No one breathed. The horror of what had just been revealed was too much to process, too much to comprehend. The courtroom was paralyzed in a state of disbelief, trapped in the moment where the truth was more terrifying than any nightmare.

A murmur rippled through the crowd, growing louder, not from the shock of the murders themselves, but from the utter audacity of hearing Mick speak it aloud. The room buzzed with disbelief, as if the words themselves were too horrific to grasp. The judge, his hand trembling slightly, gestured toward the guards who stood ten feet away from the bench, signaling them to hold back, for now. Mick, however, was far from finished. His words cut through the tension like a knife, raw and unfiltered.

"All those women... they would reject me," Mick spat, his voice thick with venom. "My fulfillment... it's complete as I watch them die." His hand struck his head repeatedly, the slap echoing in the hushed court like a drumbeat of madness. "My thoughts, my brain... there's something fucked up."

The crowd's noise escalated, a collective gasp followed by whispered exclamations of horror. Andrew Taylor, sitting in the front row, couldn't suppress a grim smile. *Oh, he's lost it,* Andrew thought, a twisted satisfaction creeping through his veins. The Devil, in his mind, had just shown up, grinning, satisfied. Anderson, on the other hand, looked as though he had aged ten years in a matter of seconds. Mick's future, would they lock him away forever, or would they put an end to it all with a death sentence?

"I have thoughts that are... unbalanced," Mick continued, his voice trembling now with a mixture of rage and something far darker. "Sometimes I just don't know. I try to feel, but I can't!" His words, desperate and jumbled, fell from his lips in a frantic burst. "All emotions are negative... after the thoughts of being rejected."

His hands shot out toward the crowd, as if reaching for the very souls in the room, his face contorting in a grotesque mask of agony and fury. "And the worst thing about this... this ceremony..." The audience fell into a tense silence, their eyes locked on him. Mick's next words broke that silence like an explosion. "When I killed Melissa... the Devil saw me do it!"

The room exploded into chaos. People in the audience shrieked, pointing, muttering in disbelief. "This guy's a fruitcake!" someone yelled. "Oh my God, those poor women..." another voice cried. "We know where this nutjob is going." The air was thick with fear, confusion, and disgust. The madness had infected them all. The court had transformed into something far darker, far more dangerous, a mob in the making, just waiting to tear him apart with their judgment.

Judge Collins nodded grimly at the guards, signaling them to move in. The weight of the moment bore down on him, but his duty was clear. Mick was beyond saving, beyond redemption. As the guards approached to cuff him, Mick's words lashed out, unrestrained, desperate. "He never made me do it," Mick raged, his eyes wild, his voice a rasp. "He just watched... just watched... said he wanted to learn more about people like me! Just fucking stood there."

The guards moved in quickly, shackling Mick's wrists with cold metal, dragging him toward his inevitable fate. As they led him away, Mick's voice rose again, trembling with a kind of twisted satisfaction. "I tried to kill the Devil... slashed him open real good, fucker winked at me as his wound healed. He was back to himself in twenty seconds."

Journalists, reporters desperate for the scoop, surged forward, shoving microphones into Mick's face, their cameras flashing. "That fucking wink..." Mick hissed through clenched teeth. "That fucking wink helped me go insane."

The guards pushed through the chaos, shoving reporters aside as they marched Mick out of the courtroom. The crowd seemed to collectively exhale, but the tension lingered in the air, thick and oppressive.

And then, at the very front of the court, there was something else, a figure, slipping quietly out the door. The Devil himself, his presence felt in the weight of every lingering word Mick had spoken. Andrew Taylor, speechless, could only watch as the man he had been thinking of, the one who had haunted Mick's every word, vanished from sight.

"Well," Andrew muttered under his breath, his thoughts heavy with an unsettling certainty. "We don't have to look for the missing women anymore."

He thought of Gary Brown and what he might say, how they would try to explain it all. *The more you talk about the Devil, the more he becomes a fantasy... and the more you speak of him, the less you believe, especially when it comes from a lunatic.*

40

Through the Cracks

The atmosphere in Judge Collins' chambers was suffocating, heavy with unspoken thoughts. The sound of glass clinking as bourbon was poured echoed through the room, but no one seemed to notice. The Prosecutors, the Defense, and Judge Collins himself were still reeling from the events of just two hours ago. A collective sense of disbelief hung in the air, each person struggling to process what they had just witnessed.

Collins, his voice calm but carrying a weight of finality, broke the silence. "Given what we've all just witnessed, we are no longer bound by the laws of this state to wait for a jury to determine Mick Enderson's fate. His confession, which everyone in this room heard, is his conviction. He is guilty."

Anderson, sitting across from the Judge, couldn't help but think of Melissa Miller, Mick's first victim. Melissa's family, immensely wealthy and controlling much of the city's power, had no need to seek justice in this case. But the question gnawed at Anderson's mind: *Did Mick deserve justice?* Or had his fate been sealed the moment his path crossed with the powerful forces that controlled the city?

Judge Collins continued, his voice unwavering. "Detective Taylor witnessed Mick holding a ball of iron, ready to kill the girl he kidnapped. And the man himself claims to have seen the Devil. Clearly, he is insane. But now, his fate lies in my hands. Does anyone have any questions?"

Anderson's mind was a whirlwind. Most of what Collins said was true. But what about the questions that remained unanswered, the ones Mick had danced around during his trial? Was his insanity plea part of a calculated move, a strategic play to ensure his survival? Anderson couldn't shake the feeling that Mick had anticipated everything. That performance in court... it wasn't just to avoid death, it was a show, a game. Why delay the inevitable?

The Prosecutors, satisfied with the results of their hard work, said nothing. This trial was a stepping stone for them, a case that would shine bright on their resumes. A serial killer brought to justice, young, eager, and ready to climb the ranks.

Judge Collins finished his bourbon with a sharp tilt of his head and moved to his desk. He pressed a button, summoning his secretary. "Get Joe Hughes on the line. I need to know the best time for an execution."

Meanwhile, Detective Andrew Taylor received an unexpected call from the detention area. "Detective Taylor," he answered, his voice steady but curious.

A guard's voice came through, hesitant but urgent. "Sir, one of the inmates, Mick Enderson, asked me to get in touch with you. He says he knows where a body is, in a river outside Ashland. He mentioned it was a place he's been to before... not sure if he's playing games or not."

Taylor's mind raced. Mick had already confessed to burning all the bodies. So why this sudden change? Was he trying to buy time? "At court, Mick said he burned them all... is he messing with us? Or you?" Taylor asked, his voice tinged with suspicion.

"I don't know, sir," the guard replied, "But he said there's one in the river. Maybe he's telling the truth, maybe not. I'm just passing the message along."

Taylor sat in silence for a moment before replying, "Thanks, I'll keep it in mind." Mick had two days left. Was this some last-ditch effort to avoid his execution?

Taylor's thoughts shifted to his next move; he needed to act fast.

He dialed Gary Weinrib's number. "Hey, Gary," Taylor greeted, his voice steady despite the brewing storm in his chest.

"Andrew! What's going on?" Gary responded, cheerful as ever.

"Do you still SCUBA dive? I've got a lead on a body in a river. Mick's claiming he knows where it is," Taylor said, his words clipped with urgency.

"A river? Sure, no problem," Gary replied, already gathering the necessary equipment in his mind.

"Can you do it today?" Andrew asked, his voice low but firm.

"I'll get my gear," Gary said. "Call you soon."

As Taylor made his way to the detention area, the weight of the situation pressed down on him. The guards let him into the interrogation room, where Mick sat, as calm as ever. Taylor couldn't help but be impressed; there was something almost regal about Mick's demeanor, despite his crimes.

"Nice to see you, Mick," Taylor said, his voice laced with a touch of irony. "That performance in court? Beautiful. Made everyone's job a lot easier."

Mick's lips curled into a slight, inscrutable smile. "Yeah," he replied slowly, his voice almost philosophical. "It's a strange thing, having all these notions in my head. I don't know how to grasp them, how to make sense of it all. People talk about voices. But they're not voices, Detective. They're just thoughts. You choose which ones to act on."

Taylor wasn't fooled. He knew how dangerous a mind like Mick's could be, calculating, manipulative, twisted. "So, Mick," he leaned in, his gaze cold and direct, "Did the Devil tell you to do all this shit? Or was it just you playing God?" "

That's how we'll make a deal, Andrew." Mick's voice was eerily calm. "I'm not going to talk to you about... that thing, my last victim, Brenda, I think her name was. I was tired of burning bodies. I wrapped her up in canvas and tossed her in the river."

Andrew's fury ignited in an instant. The words were cold, detached, as though Mick had just described a mundane task. "Listen, you sack of shit," Andrew's voice dropped to a growl. "I don't feel a damn ounce of pity for you. Every time I look at you, I think of families missing someone. You want a deal? What the hell do you want from me?"

Mick remained unshaken, his eyes dull but calculating. "Two days, Andrew. Midnight. I'm going to fry. I want a Catholic priest before my execution. Not that big of a deal, right? He'll be there anyway, but I want 20 minutes with him before... and I'll tell you where Brenda's body is."

Andrew's fury surged again. "I want Brenda NOW!" he barked, fists tightening. Mick's lips curled into a small, mocking smile. "Let's go."

Andrew stormed out of the room, grabbing his phone. "Gary, we're heading out now. One body, one river. Get another officer, follow me in the second car."

Gary's voice came through, clipped and ready. "Five minutes, we're set."

The drive was heavy with anticipation. The suspect transport enclosure in Andrew's car clinked with chains as Mick shuffled in the backseat. His hands and ankles bound, dressed in orange, his gait restricted by his restraints, Mick seemed almost calm as they sped toward their destination.

"So what's the deal, Mick? You just got tired of burning bodies?" Andrew's voice was sharp, pressing for answers.

Mick's voice was almost nonchalant. "It's a lot of work, you know? Taking apart a body. Your forensics couldn't find shit. I covered everything in plastic, burned the flesh in my fire pit. Just got tired of it. Took Brenda out for a swim," he laughed, a cold, empty sound.

Andrew gritted his teeth, fighting to keep his composure. "Was she the one who gave you that nice shiny?" he spat.

"Yeah," Mick replied, his voice almost nostalgic. "Her foot hit me right in the face, smacked off the ceiling, as I was dragging her to the backseat."

Andrew seethed. "She didn't hit you hard enough, shithead. She didn't hit you hard enough," he muttered under his breath.

The car veered onto a side road, the river visible just beyond the trees. Mick pointed, his voice lazy. "Right here. That's it."

Andrew's senses were on high alert as he stepped out of the car, gun drawn, eyes scanning for any sign of a trap. The second car pulled up behind them, the other officer stepping out, his weapon raised, ready for anything.

Andrew kept his eyes on Mick, never lowering his guard. "No one's around. No cars. No movement," he muttered, as Gary started unloading his equipment, preparing to dive. The water wasn't deep enough for an air tank, but snorkeling would do.

Mick was allowed out of the car, a gun trained on him as he led the way to the water's edge. "She should be right over there," Mick pointed, a sickening sense of finality in his tone.

Andrew kept his gun steady on Mick, making sure the other officer watched the road. Seconds stretched into eternity as they waited. The river was eerily still, the air thick with the silence of what was to come.

Gary was already under the water, his body vanishing into the depths. Andrew's gaze never left Mick, his mind racing. "Well, at least one family will have a funeral," he muttered.

Moments passed before Gary's head emerged from the water, his voice muffled as he spoke. "This is heavy." Andrew's heart pounded in his chest as Gary walked toward him, a heavy canvas bundle in his arms. He laid it down on the shore, slowly unraveling it. As the cloth came off, the first thing Andrew saw was the hair. Red hair. The unmistakable sign of Brenda.

"Redhead, huh, Mick?" Andrew's voice was a cold challenge.

Mick didn't react, his eyes dull as he stared at the body. The silence between them grew thick.

Gary looked at Andrew, his face grim. "She's the one," he said, his voice hard.

"Gary," Andrew snapped, his gaze unflinching. "You and the other officer take her to Schmidt's Funeral Home. Get her ready."

"Yes, sir," Gary replied.

Andrew turned back to Mick, his expression stone-cold.

"Let's go," he ordered, his voice devoid of emotion.

The drive back was suffocating in its silence. Neither man spoke. When they arrived at the prison, Andrew led Mick back to his cell. The clang of the door echoing as it slammed shut.

"Well, Mick," Andrew said, his voice thick with finality, "this is the last time I ever have to look at your sorry ass."

Mick's eyes flickered up, a glint of something dark in them. "The priest will come before my execution?"

Andrew didn't hesitate. "Yes. I'll make sure. The interrogation room, right before the execution room."

Mick didn't smile, didn't say a word. He simply turned and walked into his cell, the door clanging shut behind him.

41

A Killer's Undoing

It was dark, like the final moments before a thunderstorm, the weight of Mick Enderson's last day on Earth hanging in the silence. The very walls seemed to sag with a kind of sorrow, as if they, too, knew what was to come. The interrogation room was dim, faded, and ominous, like a tomb. Mick sat at the table, dressed in the harsh orange of his prison garb, his hands shackled to the cold metal. A man condemned, both in body and soul.

Outside the prison, the world moved on, indifferent. Inside, Gary Brown, the priest, approached with a heart heavy with both dread and duty. He hadn't known what to expect when Detective Taylor called him, asking him to speak to the notorious serial killer Mick Enderson. Gary's mind swirled with memories of a confession long ago, a woman named Sara, her voice trembling as she revealed the darkest of truths. Her son... Mick. The boy who had once been hers, the boy she had never understood, was the monster who now stood before him. He was the very thing she had feared. Gary had never shared her confession, not even with Mick, for it had been given in the sacred privacy of faith, whispered to Jesus Christ alone.

As Gary entered the prison, the guards barely glanced at him, their vigilance subdued as they silently acknowledged his presence. They barely searched his clothes; he was a man of God, after all. The heavy iron door behind him slammed shut with a metallic finality. "Go down the hall, Father," one of the guards muttered, his voice void of warmth. "About twenty feet. Mick's in the interrogation room on your left."

"Thank you, sir," Gary replied softly, his voice barely more than a whisper, as if to avoid disturbing the suffocating silence that seemed to swallow him whole. He glanced at his phone, 11:38 PM. The time seemed irrelevant, lost in the void of the moment.

As he stepped into the hall, a sickly darkness crept along the edges of his vision, an unnatural shadow that swallowed the flickers of light above. Each step he took seemed to drag him further into a place devoid of hope, a place where sorrow and despair reigned supreme. The hallway stretched out before him like the mouth of a vast, endless abyss. He was walking into the very heart of nothingness.

At the end of the hall, he saw the guard standing outside the door, his hands clasped behind his back. His expression was blank, devoid of any emotion, as if he, too, had succumbed to the darkness that filled the air. Gary's footsteps faltered as he drew nearer, a chilling sense of foreboding gripping his chest.

The door creaked open, and there he was, Mick. His eyes locked onto Gary with an unsettling intensity, a look that could only be described as predatory. He didn't smile. He didn't grin. But his expression twisted in something between both, a mockery of human warmth.

"Thank you, Father," Mick said, his voice low, almost amused. "I need to talk to a priest... for my sins."

Gary tried to force a sense of calm, to steady the storm in his chest. "Hello, Mick," he said, his tone as cordial as he could muster. "I don't really know what you need, but if this is a confession, we should be at the Church." He moved toward the table and took a seat, his eyes never leaving Mick's.

He couldn't help but think: *He's so young. So very young, and yet... the weight in his eyes makes him seem a lifetime older.*

Mick's lips twitched, a strange, nervous tic as a single tear slid down his left cheek. Gary's gaze shifted, but he couldn't look away from the unrelenting darkness that swam in those eyes.

"Well... this isn't really a confession," Mick drawled, his voice tinged with bitterness, "more like a question or two. Ha... a confession? It'd take a while." He leaned back in his chair, the handcuffs clinking against the metal. "Of the girls I... killed... well, I wouldn't want to get too deliberate about it. My methods... my brain told me it was necessary. They shamed me. Rejected me. When I was done with them... they couldn't shame me anymore."

Gary's voice was steady, but the words cut through the thick air like a blade. "On the contrary, Mick," he said firmly, "it sounds like you need a true confession."

Mick's whole body jerked, as if the suggestion had struck him like a physical blow. He bellowed in response, his voice raw and guttural. "No, Priest... I said I have questions, not confessions!" His words echoed through the bleak room. The guard glanced in, but Gary remained unfazed, locking eyes with Mick. "It's alright," Gary reassured, though his own heart was racing.

Mick's gaze faltered, and for the first time, his mask cracked. He dropped his head, his voice barely audible. "I'm sorry, Priest."

Gary's eyes softened. "You can call me Gary."

"No... Priest is better for me," Mick muttered, as though the title gave him some twisted form of comfort.

Gary felt an oppressive weight settle over him. The darkness in Mick's words had infected the room, swallowing him whole. His defenses were faltering. *This is not what I thought it would be like,* he thought, feeling the enormity of the situation crash over him.

Mick continued, his voice trembling but growing in intensity. "I've done so many... cynical and questionable things," he spat. "I had one of my victims' heads in my bedroom. I liked the look on her face. But the smell... the smell was intolerable. I burned the flesh and chiseled her skull to powder. I worked so hard to leave no proof, no trace. I took care of their bodies... their flesh." His words hung in the air like a vile stench.

Gary's senses dulled, the reality of Mick's depravity overwhelming him. He had hoped time would numb the horror, but it only deepened. *I can't... I can't stand this,* he thought.

Mick's eyes glinted with a dark revelation. "I don't know if you're aware, but I kept track of their hair color in a notebook. I noted it all down, like a twisted diary on my desk. They used that against me," he muttered, a bitter laugh escaping him. "I'm stupid sometimes... I should never have done that."

Gary had braced himself for something like this. He could feel it, the storm of darkness that would never relent. "I feel for you, son," he said, his voice quiet yet resolute. "Are you asking for forgiveness from our Savior, Jesus Christ?"

Mick looked up at him, his eyes wide with a strange, unholy intensity. "For what I've done? Would you forgive me, Priest?"

Gary's chest tightened as he spoke the words he had hoped would never come. "Through reckoning, forgiveness asked of Christ... yes, I would. The highest blasphemy against the Holy Spirit can be cleansed through our Savior."

Mick let out a mocking chuckle, his grin chilling. "How faithful you are, Priest... maybe there's a chance for me after all. But you still don't understand, do you? Most of my victims were unconscious... that's good, isn't it? I'd hammer them with my ball..." His words trailed off, too horrid to finish. "I raped one or two of them... they moaned, mostly unaware."

Gary's heart pounded in his chest, the shock of Mick's words shattering any pretense of normalcy. His mind screamed for release, for something to make sense of this nightmare. *Deal with it*, he told himself. *He's a killer. He needs a confession. Maybe this is the best for him. Maybe God will save him.*

Mick closed his eyes, his face contorting with emotion. "I thought all these women would reject me, use me, and throw me away like trash," he whispered, as though revealing the deepest truth about his soul. "That thought haunted me, constantly. And then... I got tired of it. So tired... so very tired of it." His voice cracked, a bitter breath escaping his lungs. He lowered his head, defeated. "But... I will get you to the real reason I asked for you, Priest. On your faith, Priest... do you believe in heaven and hell? God and the Devil?"

Gary didn't hesitate. "Yes, Mick. My faith and belief are pure."

Mick's eyes shone with something unnatural, as if the very air around them had thickened with a malevolent force. "When I... killed Melissa," he whispered, "my first victim... I had so many things in mind to do to her body. So beautiful... so gracious... But something happened." His words were thick with dark reverence, as though the memory itself was alive and breathing.

Gary leaned forward, sensing that Mick was about to reveal something unspeakable. "What, my son?" he asked, his voice laced with caution.

Mick's breath hitched, his eyes wide with a mixture of fear and mania. "I had her naked... on my couch... and someone was there," he muttered, almost afraid to say it aloud.

Gary's brow furrowed in confusion. "Um... other than you two?" he asked, his voice trembling despite himself.

Mick's gaze shifted, as though listening for an answer from somewhere beyond the room. "Did you read the papers about this? About my work?" Mick asked, his voice rising with anticipation.

Gary swallowed hard, his mind reeling. "Yes, I read a portion of it. You saw something, or imagined something, perhaps."

Mick's lips curled into something sinister. "Yes... someone was there. I told everyone in court the truth," he hissed, as if sharing an occult secret. "The other person was... the Devil."

Gary recoiled, a cold shiver running through him. "The Devil... saw you do this?" he whispered, almost afraid to speak the words aloud.

Mick's shriek broke the air like a crack of thunder, echoing through the room. "The Devil was there... watched me kill Melissa!" he cried, his voice now raw with hysteria.

Outside, the guard remained motionless, unmoved by the scene unfolding before him. To him, Mick was not just a killer; he was insane.

Gary's heart seemed to stop. "Oh my God," he whispered, the words a prayer, a gasp, a plea all at once.

Mick's voice erupted, wild and frantic, as he shouted, "Listen! I'm not stupid! I thought he was a burglar, or something, someone who broke into my house. So I figured I'd teach that asshole a lesson he'd never forget. I took my hunter's knife, the same one I used on Melissa, and I split his neck wide open. A huge gash, ear to ear. That bastard smiled at me! Smiled and winked at me, even as the cut closed up right in front of my eyes! He said he wanted to learn about people like me... or something like that. He wasn't human, Gary! Do you understand me?!"

Gary stood silent for a moment, the words ringing in his ears, cutting deeper than any confession. "You should have told the authorities this before trial, Mick," he said softly, his voice tinged with regret. "It could have saved your life. Reasonable doubt... not guilty by insanity."

Mick's voice dropped into a guttural rasp, as if the weight of his confession threatened to crush him from the inside. "I have nightmares... or maybe it's worse than that. The Devil's always there, watching me, tormenting me. It's been like this since Melissa. That wink, Gary... it's what drove me insane."

Just then, a heavy silence filled the room, followed by the unmistakable sound of boots on the floor. The door swung open, revealing a tall man in a cowboy hat, flanked by two guards. "It's time, Mick," the man said, his voice flat and devoid of empathy.

"Yeah... finally," Mick muttered, the venom in his words dripping with a mix of anger and dread. "About God damn time."

The group of five filed out into the hallway, the sound of their footsteps echoing through the corridor. Gary, lost in thought, whispered prayers under his breath as they made their way down the sterile halls to the execution room. The stark fluorescent lights above seemed to buzz with an unnatural hum, intensifying the tension that hung in the air.

As they entered the execution chamber, two men dressed as nurses were busy preparing the equipment.

A table, stark and cold like an altar, awaited Mick. It was positioned like a cross, its cruel shape designed to hold him in place. One guard and a nurse carefully helped Mick onto the table, strapping him in as though preparing him for a sacrificial ritual. The other nurse reached over to pull a blindfold from the other side of the room, the glass walls letting the world beyond watch the gruesome spectacle unfold, journalists, reporters, and the families of the victims all poised in judgment.

And there, standing just beyond the glass, was a figure in a three-piece suit, a bowler hat perched jauntily atop his head. He leaned heavily on a cane, both hands clasped around it like some twisted symbol of power. His eyes met Mick's through the glass. He winked.

Mick's face contorted with horror, his voice cracking. "Oh shit!" he screamed, panic flooding his every pore. "Oh, fucking hell!" His body thrashed against the restraints as he was strapped down tighter, terror flooding his eyes. "The Devil is right there!" he bellowed, his voice laced with raw fear. "Can't you see him? He's right there on the other side of the glass! He's fucking winking at me!"

The man in the cowboy hat spoke, his voice cold and indifferent. "Let's hurry up. Let's get this done."

The nurses, moving with mechanical precision, inserted the needle into Mick's arm, and within moments, the poison began its deadly work. Mick's body jerked, convulsing as the chemical venom coursed through his veins. The world seemed to slow for him, the sharp sting of fear cutting deeper than the pain in his arm.

And then, that smile, no, that wink, the Devil's grin that had haunted him since that night with Melissa, that twisted, sinful smile that never left his mind. Mick's voice trembled, broken with despair, his last words a tortured cry. "Oh God... that fucking wink... that God damn wink..." His words were a strangled plea, lost in the growing haze of poison. "Oh... help... help me...!"

As Mick's body grew limp, the life draining from him, Gary, standing at the foot of the table, leaned in, his voice a soft murmur amidst the suffocating silence. "I commend you, my brother. From earth to dust, Holy Mary and the Angels, this man needs God's help."

And just like that, Mick's breath slowed. His body went still, the weight of his sins now a permanent, unshakeable mark on his soul.

---

www.ingramcontent.com/pod-product-compliance
Lightning Source LLC
LaVergne TN
LVHW020543070326
833226LV00013B/300